Letters
from the
Heart

Letters from the Heart

1943-1946

CAROLE WEBB SLATER

authorHOUSE®

AuthorHouse™
1663 Liberty Drive
Bloomington, IN 47403
www.authorhouse.com
Phone: 1-800-839-8640

Published by AuthorHouse   05/08/2013

ISBN: 978-1-4817-2753-2 (sc)
ISBN: 978-1-4817-2752-5 (hc)
ISBN: 978-1-4817-2751-8 (e)

Library of Congress Control Number: 2013906740

Contents

"If I can stay on the beam . . . I'll be 'in.'"

This book is dedicated to my family for inspiration and support, and to my father and mother, Cobby and Evey, who instilled love of family, love of country, and love of life in the hearts of all of us.

FOREWORD

This book is about family and when we are touched by love we are given a priceless gift that becomes a part of who we are in this life.

Cobby was my older brother and all my life I wanted to be like him. In my hometown of St. Albans, my dad was "old Cobby", my brother was "young Cobby" and, since I was six years younger, I was "baby Cobby." Growing up I played football, basketball, and baseball to be like Cobby, I became a mechanical engineer because Cobby was an aeronautical engineer, I became a fighter pilot [during the Korean conflict} because Cobby was a fighter pilot. In fact, I was the last family member to see him alive before he was killed in a training exercise flying a F-84 E fighter plane. Oddly enough, on the day he died I was on a cross-country flight in an identical airplane. I remember most the wonderful years that we spent together at the University of Kentucky. Carole's book tells about his love, his life, his family and how much we all miss him. God bless anyone who reads this book and all who played a part in young Cobby's life. *Clayton Eugene Webb*

Mike and I were five years old when Dad died. As I was growing up, there were stories about Dad and some worn black and white photographs but I didn't know what was important to him or understand his perspectives. Through this book of letters, I have seen into the heart of this man and now that vision of my Dad is in living color. His thoughts and attitudes about life are so familiar and I have seen parts of myself in these letters. It has been a great thrill knowing we share these common traits. It was my privilege to serve my country in the U.S.A.F. as a fighter pilot in the F-106. My years as a pilot were exhilarating as flying seemed natural because I felt Dad was always there with his hand on that stick every time I flew. *Patrick Eugene "Webb" Moore.*

Helping my sister with this unique book project was like getting to know my dad for the first time. As a career Fighter Pilot, and retired Air Force Officer, reading these personal letters from my "long lost hero", was like opening up my soul and seeing for the first time "why" my life had taken this path. I have flown F-4 Phantoms and F-15 Eagles all over the world, and deep in my heart I never fully understood why I chose this particular life. I now realize, that Cobby's blood flows in my veins, and I never really had a choice. I am a Webb by birth and D.A.Webb was my father! Thank you Carole for giving me my dad again. *Michael Dana "Webb" Moore (aka Moose), Fighter Pilot and son of Cobby.*

INTRODUCTION

Letters from the Heart is the story of Dana A. Webb, Jr., "Cobby,", a P-51 pilot, assigned to the 328th Fighter Squadron and the 352nd Fighter Group stationed in England and Belgium during World War II. Cobby was born in January, 1924, and was twenty years old when he went off to war.

This is a work of nonfiction based primarily on letters written by Cobby Webb to his parents and his girlfriend, Evelyn, who later became his wife, with occasional letters written by Evelyn to Cobby's parents. There are more than two hundred fifty letters telling the story of a young pilot in training and in war, a son devoted to his family, and the love between a man and woman who meet by chance and find magic that lasts a lifetime. The letters herein were transcribed as they were spontaneously written by Cobby and Evelyn, maintaining the integrity of the hand-written text, reflecting the vernacular of the times, and capturing grammatical inaccuracies. In some instances slight changes to wording and corrections to punctuation were made to ensure ease of reading.

In addition, there are other types of memorabilia, such as newspaper clippings, telegrams from Western Union, V-Mail letters, brochures about Army Aviation Cadet training, pictures of airplanes Cobby flew in training, descriptions of different flight training sites, as well as historical references relating to an event occurring during 1940s wartime and mentioned in a letter.

World War II, unlike other wars since, brought the United States of America together as a country, united for the good of all. The generation of men and women who grew up during the Great Depression and went on to fight in World War II or contribute on the home front became known as "The Greatest Generation." They sacrificed and fought because it was the right thing to do, and afterward, they rebuilt America into a world power.

This book holds the experiences, feelings, and words of two of America's greatest generation.

CHAPTER ONE

Secret Treasures of My Mother's Heart, 1988

I opened the chest, and the pungent scent of cedar filled my nostrils as I sat cross-legged on the raw wood floor under beams that angled up and held my house together.

I inherited this cedar trunk when my mother died unexpectedly in November, 1985. It was not an unusual or attractive piece of furniture. In fact, it was a plain, old, rectangular, wooden chest that was heavy and bulky. Although my mother never talked about this chest, I knew intuitively that it was meant for me. I sensed the chest was an important tie to my mother's life, although I really didn't know why. My husband and brothers moved it from my mother's house to mine, and even though I was curious about its contents, I stored it in the attic and avoided opening it for three years. The sudden loss of my mother to a heart attack when she was sixty was shocking and painful, and in my grief I was not able to handle her belongings.

It was also a hectic time, and I had other distractions that enriched my life. I was married to a good man and was now a mother, too, and I stayed busy tending to my daughter, age three, named Ruth after my mother, whose name was Ruth Evelyn, and my two-year-old son, Dana, named after my father. I also worked thirty hours a week at Vanderbilt Hospital in Nashville and created a balance of quality time with my children and family while working outside the home. The days went by in a blur.

On this chilly, fall, Sunday afternoon, I decided I was ready to see what my mother kept in this mystery chest that I knew so little about.

It was half full and held an autograph book from my mother's teen years and a 1941 East High School annual from her senior year. I sorted through hand-stitched towels, crocheted doilies, and a completed stitched flower design from a crewel embroidery kit, all in perfect condition. In awe, I realized this must be my mother's hope chest, given to her by her parents when she became engaged to my father in 1944.

1944. The world was deeply entrenched in World War II, and I knew my father was a P-51 pilot stationed in Europe during this time.

Under the handmade items in the trunk were my baby book from 1948 and a framed baby photo of me with hand-painted, soft pink cheeks and a carefully arranged lock of real hair in a curl pasted on my head. I came along three years after the war. I found several pairs of keepsake bronzed baby shoes and two cloth soldier dolls in good condition that belonged to my younger twin brothers. Suddenly, I was filled with a longing for my mother.

At the bottom of the trunk I found three shoe boxes tied neatly with ribbon. The cardboard was worn and had ragged edges. I untied the string around one of the boxes, lifted the lid, and found letters addressed to my mother. Instinctively, I knew who had written them. I lifted the boxes out of the trunk, flipped through a stack, and looked at the return addresses—Flight 17, Keesler Field, Mississippi; Squadron F-2, Nashville, Tennessee; Craig Field, Selma, Alabama; Perry Army Air Field, Perry, Florida. There were two hundred fifty letters in the boxes, all postmarked in the 1940s, all still in good condition as if waiting to be found. My heart skipped because I knew instinctively that they were the words of my father. I picked out a few to read.

> **Golly, Ev, I wanta see you so darn bad it hurts. I can't even begin to tell you how much I love you in these letters.**

11 February 1944

The letters would tell a story of the day my father met my mother at a USO-sponsored dance at the YMCA in Nashville, his journey through flight training, and his travels overseas as a fighter pilot during the war.

> **I have a secret ambition to fly a P-51 Mustang. Man alive, give me one of those and a couple of good wing men, and lookout Luftwaffe.**

23 March 1944

> **I start night flying tonight, and if I can stay on the beam and not have any accidents I'll be "in." Now, if I'm made a Flight Officer, I'll be just about the happiest guy in the world. Wings and bars, a furlough slip in my pocket and on my way to see the most wonderful gal in the world.**

28 February 1944

My intuitions had been correct. This trunk was a very special secret of my mother's heart that she kept safely hidden away. I began to cry. My mother had kept these letters for over thirty years as a reminder of a love that even death could not end.

I don't know how I can tell you how much I love you, after having you in my arms just two short days ago . . . Golly, baby, I feel like a new man, no kiddin' . . . I go around telling all the guys I know that I'm engaged . . . to the sweetest girl in the whole world.

15 March 1944

My father trained at different air fields in the South, then was assigned to the 328th Fighter Squadron and the 352nd Fighter Group stationed in England and later Belgium during the war. These letters must have sustained my mother and held her together during the war years and after her husband's untimely death ten years later.

I think about what I'm going to do after the war. If I make the grade and get my wings and outlive the war, I'm going to try and get a connection with an airline . . . I'd sure like to retire after the war and just love you!

15 March 1944

Cobby was thirty-one years old when he died on June 25, 1955, in a horrific airplane crash while flying on a weekend mission with the Ohio National Guard. He worked as an aeronautical engineer at Wright Patterson Air Force Base and lived with his eyes on the sky. My mother, brothers, and I were visiting my grandparents in St. Albans, West Virginia, that day. I was seven years old, and my twin brothers were barely five, when our mother received that unexpected, life-changing call.

An experienced fighter pilot, my father had survived the terrible war in Europe, which made his death more of an unbelievable shock. The grief settled in my mother's heart where it stayed tucked away inside.

Life went on. My mother moved her family to her hometown of Nashville to be close to her parents and found a part-time typing job she could do from home. She was not prepared to work outside the home, so the next few years we lived on savings and life insurance payments in a small two-bedroom rental house down the street from my grandparents.

Eventually, my mother remarried, and changes occurred again in our lives, as she tried to carve out a new family that would include a wonderful little sister. But it was clear that my mother married for convenience and financial security for her children, and over the years she focused on raising us, finding satisfaction in volunteer work, and nurturing relationships with a circle of women friends.

I believe the threads of joy found in her memories of love helped sustain her as the years went by, and this love was shared with us in ways other than personal stories and black-and-white photographs. My mother's eyes sparkled when she talked of our father. I could hear happiness in her laughter as she recalled funny incidents that happened and devotion in her voice as she spoke about Cobby. I could feel the love. My mother savored her memories with my father and often talked of feeling lucky to have found such a great love for eleven wonderful years.

My brothers grew up to be what my mother referred to as a "combination of our father." Pat had his tall, lanky build, full lips, and fun-loving personality, while twin brother Mike, better known as Moose, was shorter with broad shoulders, our dad's same blondish hair, sky-blue eyes, a big infectious grin, and joy for living life fully. Both brothers, like our father, grew up knowing that flying airplanes would be part of their future. After college they both joined the U.S. Air Force. Pat flew the F-106 Interceptor for several years, and Mike stayed in for twenty years where he flew his dream plane, the F-15 Eagle, while serving as Operations Officer of the 94th Tactical Fighter Squadron. The love of flying airplanes was in their blood and connected them to the heart of our father and mother.

I didn't have that connection. But now I had these letters, and I couldn't wait to tell my brothers.

I moved my treasure boxes from the attic and contemplated what I would do with them. I collected more letters from Cobby's mother, Fritzi, who had kept newspaper clippings from war time, brochures from flight training sites, and letters her son had written home to her. I organized and sorted all the letters in chronological order. A pattern emerged, and I noticed there were often two or three letters written each week.

I read them all and discovered, to my profound delight, that my father's letters were straight from the heart and told the story of his life and the times. A story of a nineteen-year-old man who gave up his football scholarship at Miami of Ohio University to join the United States Army Air Corp to fight for his country in World War II. A story about a family and how values of honor and responsibility learned at home were lived out in a war. A story about a man who found true love. This is a story rich with historical events, places, and people that rocked our world, and a remarkable time in history when Americans were united in support of their country.

But for me, these letters tell a story that brought my dad to life again.

And these letters will give my children—my parents' namesakes—understanding of the substance of their foundation and will show all the family what we're built on and what will always hold us tightly together as the generations pass.

CHAPTER TWO

On the Homefront, 1943

Cobby Webb grew up in St. Albans, a small industrial town of 2,500 residents in West Virginia. He lived with his parents and younger brother, Clayton, in a house his parents built right after their marriage in the early 1920's and where his mother would live for seventy years. The interior style and furnishings of this two-story clapboard house, last updated in the 1950's, would remain unchanged until his mother moved out in the 1990's at ninety-three years of age.

"Mom, Clayton and I in the early years" [Cobby Webb]

"Mom, Pop and Clayton 'at home' in 1944" [Cobby Webb]

Cobby's father, Dana Algernon Webb, Sr., or "Cob Web" to his friends and "Pop" to his children, was a serious man who worked late hours as a yardmaster at the Chesapeake & Ohio (C&O) train depot in town. Cobby was more like his gregarious, outspoken, and independent-minded mother. Frances "Fritzi" McClung Webb, with flaming red hair, graduated in 1918 from Marshall College, participated in the local St. Albans suffragette movement, and on the personal side, loved to dance, play cards, play golf, and smoke cigarettes (in secret places). Fritzi was also a traditional wife—at least she tried to be—and a devoted mother to her two sons.

Cobby inherited her independent outgoing personality and determination to succeed on his own terms. A graduate of St. Albans High School in 1941, he wrote in his annual that his future was in aeronautical engineering because he had always been interested in airplanes and speed. A natural athlete, Cobby loved playing all sports, but football would provide him with a college scholarship to Miami of Ohio University in Oxford, Ohio. Cobby entered Miami of Ohio University in the fall of 1942 and played first string football that season, but he felt a growing sense of responsibility to his country and the war being fought against Germany and Japan. Cobby dropped out of school after the fall semester and exchanged his Miami football uniform for a different one with the newly formed United States Army Air Corps. In February 1943, the Webb family, with a proud and heavy heart filled with mixed emotions, said goodbye to their beloved first-born son, understanding that Cobby's future was uncertain with life or death in the balance.

Life in America was changing rapidly as families sent their loved ones off to war and all citizens, young and old, prepared to make sacrifices for their country. Major changes occurred in neighborhoods, at local factories, in retail stores, with many programs spearheaded by volunteers and guided by government policies and regulations supported by citizens across the country. As factories converted to military defense industries, fewer manufactured goods were available, creating shortages of supply. The government created a system of rationing items in short supply while establishing price controls to keep down the prices. War ration books and tokens were issued to each American family, dictating how much gasoline, tires, sugar, meat, silk, shoes, nylon, and other items that any one person could buy. Food rationing affected Americans the most. Families were encouraged to plant victory gardens to help with food supply shortages. Rubber and gas were the most vital products rationed, and civilians helped by organizing scrap drives of recycled materials that contained metal, steel, or rubber. Another opportunity for civilians to support the troops was through the purchase of war bonds. When a person bought a war bond, the federal government promised to pay that person's money back plus interest in a certain number of years. The government then used money from bonds sales to help pay for war costs like building ships and airplanes. The bonds allowed citizens to loan money to the government to help financially support the war effort. Even the United States Congress stayed busy working together to pass laws on behalf of Americans rather than stonewalling or perpetuating an ideology of either political party persuasion.

There were other major changes occurring in the workplace. World War II ironically ended the Great Depression with seventeen million new jobs in war-related industries, creating a booming time of unparalleled economic growth. With so many men fighting in the war, women were hired for jobs previously held by men, such as riveters, welders, and inspectors, creating a dramatic change of a woman's role in the workplace.

The United States was a country united by a common purpose, and it was an unprecedented time in American history.

REFERENCES

[1] Top Story: Life, even at home, changed for everyone during World War II." *The Herald—Dispatch*. 15 January 2009. Accessed September 15, 2012. http://www.herald-dispatch.com/specialsections/100years/x613396121/ TOP-STORY-Life-even-at-home-changed-for-everyone-during- World- War-II.

[2] "Tennessee 4 Me, WWII." Tennessee State Museum. Accessed July 10, 2012. http://www.tn4me.org/major_cat.cfm/major_id/9/era_id/7.

[3] *World War II and the American Homefront*. (2004) National Historic Landmarks Program of the National Park Service. Accessed July 10, 2012. http://www.nps.gov/nhl/themes/ homefrontstudy.pdf

CHAPTER THREE

Joining U.S. Army Air Forces, February 1943

In 1941 the Army Air Force (AAF) was created by Congress to add an aviation element, equal to the Army ground forces, which would later become the U.S. Air Force. By December of this year, the AAF had grown to 354,000 men (9,000 pilots) as compared to 26,000 men (2,000 pilots) in 1939. Training schools were growing at such a rapid rate that civilian pilots and contractors were selected to operate some of the newly established flying schools. Becoming a pilot took twelve to fifteen months and was a challenging and dangerous program to complete. From 1941 to 1945, approximately forty percent of aviation cadets "washed out" and/or were killed in training. To "wash out" meant they were dismissed from the corps because they were unable to meet the requirements.

The following U.S. Army Aviation Cadets Guide, found in Cobby's personal items, was a great example of an effective marketing strategy to a group of men (and women) from the "greatest generation." The attributes in this guide were often terms used to define this generation and define an American hero. An aviation cadet must be intelligent, honorable, ethical, educated, honest, and exceptional in order to belong to this elite group of warriors in the sky. However, the requirement that a cadet must have twelve teeth distorted my mental image, ever so slightly, of an average aviation cadet. With that said, Cobby had all of his teeth, attended college, and possessed the best attributes described in this brochure and in my eyes was an American hero.

U.S. ARMY AVIATION CADETS GUIDE
"Keep'em Flying"

AVIATION AS A CAREER

Modern war has proved that no nation can exist without an adequate, well-trained air force. The basis of every air force and the characteristic upon which it succeeds or fails is the individual excellence of its flying officers and their equipment. With these two things in mind, your Nation has produced a system of aviation training which is unexcelled anywhere in the world. The men who have completed the training come from all walks of life. They have, however, several things in common. They are intelligent, of excellent character, of splendid physique, and in excellent health. They have their eyes on the skies. They have the fire and the courage which, from the days of the pioneers, have made this Nation great.

To meet the need for competent flying officers, the Army Air Corps maintains schools where training is given to aviation cadets at Government expense. This course of training is the finest anywhere in the world, and the student is paid a salary while learning.

AVIATION CADETS

Civilian candidates who are accepted for aviation cadet training in the Air Corps are enlisted as privates in the Air Corps and immediately appointed "aviation cadets." The aviation cadets constitute a body of young men who are noted for their character and excellent discipline. The pay of aviation cadets is $75 per month, with an additional $1.00 per day for subsistence, and while undergoing training, they are furnished quarters, medical care, hospitalization, necessary uniforms, clothing, equipment and a $10,000 Government Life Insurance policy, all at Government expense.

REQUIREMENTS FOR AVIATION CADET APPOINTMENT

General.—Young men who are enlisted men in the Army, or civilians, between the ages of 18 and 26 inclusive, who have been citizens of the United States for at least 10 years. Married men are eligible provided they sign a statement that dependents have sufficient means of support.

Physical.—Candidates must meet all the physical requirement as Reserve officers, except that visual acuity must be 20/20 and color vision must be normal; hearing 20/20 each ear; a stable equilibrium; good respiratory ventilation and vital capacity; a sound cardiovascular system, nervous and organic; a well-formed and coordinated physique; height minimum 60 inches, maximum 76 inches; and an integrated and stable central nervous system, combined with a temperamental constitution suitable for military aviation. No candidate will be accepted unless he has a minimum of 12 teeth, 3 pairs each of serviceable natural, opposing incisors and masticating teeth.

13

Mental.—Candidates must be able to pass a screening test designed to determine whether or not the applicant has sufficient education to enable him to absorb and comprehend the technical instruction of the aviation cadet course. Formal schooling is not a prerequisite.

THE AVIATION CADET TRAINING PROGRAM

One necessary qualification of the aviation cadet is quickness in comprehending instructions and accuracy in following directions. This ability to comprehend and to follow directions will depend in large part upon his vocabulary, his ability to understand the exact meaning of words and explanations. An examination will be given to measure the types of proficiency and in problem solving which are typical of those required in Air Corps training schools.

The aviation cadet must be able to read intelligently from Army manuals, technical manuals, and other sources, and understand what he reads.

Military flying requires a careful planning and a skillful execution of definite missions. Skill and accuracy in fundamental mathematics are essential and the aviation cadet should possess the ability to solve problems involving proportions, fractions, ratios, decimals, formulas, elementary algebra, and also be able to read and interpret graphs, tables, and charts.

The Air Corps aviation cadet training program consists of Technical School, Armament Training School, and Classification School. Pilot training will include Primary Flying School, Basic Flying School, Advanced Flying School and Transition Training before an assignment is made. Candidates eliminated from any of these types of training will be eligible to enter training in one of the other courses of Air Corps training, provided they are so recommended and that Air Corps policies permit such further training.

GRADUATION AND COMMISSION

Upon successful completion of training, aviation cadets are graduated and commissioned second lieutenants. The total pay for the newly commissioned officer is $245 per month.

Webb Ordered to Ft. Benjamin
Harrison

(St. Albans *Gazette*, February 1943)

"Cobby Webb, Jr., has received
orders to report to Fort Benjamin
Harrison, February 21st, to active
duty as Aviation Cadet in the U.S.
Army Air Forces. He graduated from
St. Albans High School in the class
of 1941, where he was letterman
in both football and basketball
his junior and senior years, and
later attended Greenbrier Military
School winning letters in the two
major sports. Cobby was at present
enrolled at Miami University, Oxford
Ohio and a recent pledge to the Delta
Tau Delta fraternity on the campus
of that school. He had received much
prominent attention for his stellar
play as first string end on Miami's
football team this past season."

Fort Benjamin Harrison served as an induction and logistical support
center where cadets were processed and ordered out to basic training
programs. After induction, Private Cobby Webb was sent to the U.S. Army
Corps Technical Center at Keesler Field in Biloxi, Mississippi.

At Keesler, basic training lasted four weeks and trains passed through
Keesler daily, dropping off new trainees and picking up graduates.
Cobby's letters to his parents began from Keesler Air Field.

February 23, 1943

Dearest Family,

Well, I've finally arrived at my destination. Got
here this morning at 3:00 after a train ride in Day
Coaches for 34 hours. There were 500 of us on a
regular troop train from Fort Benjamin. The trip
on the train was just like a football trip, everybody
cutting up and raising hell in general. I haven't done
a thing all day but stand in line and eat. Every time I
turn around, we're marching to mess. The food's pretty
good, but nothing extra.

I've heard so many different stories from washed
out cadets. They all claim that you're washed out for
the least provocation. As yet I'm forgetting everything
I hear and I'm going to mind my own business and
look out for myself. I still don't realize that I'm in the
army but give me a couple of weeks, and I'll know all
right.

It's a beautiful day and I'm sitting out in the warm
sun writing. I haven't had a bath since I left. I've only
washed once so you can imagine what I look like.
My clothes look terrible and awful dirty. I hope that
we hurry up and get assigned barracks because I feel
terrible.

Well, I gotta write more letters so I'll close. Write
again soon (to Pvt. Dana Webb) Love, Cob

February 29, 1943

Dearest Family,

Here it is Sunday, and I just got through unloading
two trucks full of mattresses. We got our uniforms the
other day, but the only thing we wear is fatigues. So far
I really like this man's army. All the guys in my hut are
swell fellows and we all get along swell.

We got shots yesterday, a typhoid, tetanus, and a vaccination, all at the same time. My arm got pretty sore, but it's OK. We also had our physical, which I had no problem breezing through. We were shown pictures on venereal diseases, and some of the cases were terrible. After that, we got the Articles of War read to us. It sure was dull, and half the guys went to sleep, but I didn't, because the ones who went to sleep had to clean up the lecture hall. Everybody here now talks about the upcoming mental exams and preflight training. They say most of the cadets wash out on the psychology tests that are given in Nashville. I'm pretty worried about that. I sure hope I can make it. It would just about kill me if I didn't make the grade.

The latest rumor is that we have 15 months of training to get our wings. I think we're going to take physics and lots of math. We have to learn Morse Code and have to be able to take 6 words a minute. We had our classification exams the other day and were interviewed today by men to find out our life history. I weigh about 180 now stripped and eating like a horse. Man, this is the life, three squares a day, a place to sleep, 50 bucks a month and damn little work, which is the important thing!

Mail call just went. NO MAIL! Say folks, whenever you send mail, send it air mail, only 6 cents. By the way, how about sending me some dough? I'm flat broke and only have 40 cents. There's so much stuff you can buy around here. I've bought a pair of sunglasses for $6.00, but boy, are they sharp and then there's trinkets, cigarettes, etc. Well, so long, I'll write again soon. All my love, Cobby

March 10, 1943

Dearest Family,

I got your packages yesterday and the money you sent, and you don't know how much I appreciate them. They're really swell and make me feel as though I am important.

I opened the cake and passed it around. It didn't last five minutes. Boy, was it good, and I sure needed cigarettes, and candy is always appreciated. Boy, talk about a guy being blue, I sure was a blue kid last night. We were all lying in bed after lights out and talking about our families and girl friends. I was telling all the fellows about my last few days at home, and how you all came to Cincy with me. I was thinking how terrible I felt about having to leave and how I almost choked up when I saw Mom start to slip, and how I had to hurry out to the train to ease things. I felt as bad just thinking about it, a big lump rose in my throat, and I had to blink back tears, and here I thought I was a man. All of the time I've been away at school, I've never been so blue before. I'm OK now.

We really started marching in earnest the first of this week and every day we drill for 3 ½ hours in the morning and 4 hours in the afternoon, and we drill all that time, except for an hour in the morning and an hour in the afternoon, when we exercise. Today was very bad hot and dusty and I'm about dead now with fatigue. But I'm getting a good tan on my face, and my muscles are getting hard. The next time you see me, I'll be a man and not a boy anymore. All my love, Cobby

March 21, 1943

Dearest Family,
   I'm sorry that I haven't written before now, but I've been terribly busy this week. A General Marshall is going to be here Monday to review all the troops stationed on this field. Yesterday we had a big dress review with about 23,000 or 30,000 men. It took us all morning, and all the fighter planes stationed here (about 15) took off and flew in formation. It was very impressive and inspiring. We've been policing the area, scrubbing our barracks, etc. because he's going to make an inspection also.
   We got paid this week and all we got was $40. I've taken out insurance—$10,000, and I'm sending home the receipt. I'm also sending $25 of my pay for you all, for the money you've sent me. All my love, Cobby

   To Cobby and others at this time, General George Marshall was "a general"—a military leader of the time. Not until after the war would history describe the importance of General Marshall and all that he accomplished as President Franklin D. Roosevelt's Army Chief of Staff during the war. Winston Churchill referred to General Marshall as the "organizer of the Allied victory," and his responsibilities to soldiers abroad and at home, including preparing the U.S. Army and new branch of the Army Air Corps for war, were very impressive. Following the war, General George Marshall was most commonly associated with the "Marshall Plan," or re-building of Europe economically, for which he won the Nobel Peace Prize in December 1953.
   Four weeks of basic training went by fast, and the next stop for Cobby was at Armament Training School, located at Transylvania College in Lexington, Kentucky. Cobby was stationed in Transylvania for several months, attending classes on a college campus, learning about military weapons, and studying math, physics, and history.

May 27, 1943

Dearest Family,

Boy, I'm sure glad you all got to come down here to see me. I sure had a wonderful week-end. I hope you all enjoyed it as much as I did.

Well, I started flying on time Monday. I got forty minutes flying time. It was a beautiful clear day, not a cloud in the sky, and ceiling unlimited. The instructor let me take off, I mean let me follow him on the controls. When we reached 400 feet we did a 90-degree turn to the left out of traffic then immediately afterward did a 45-degree climbing turn to the right and leveled off at 500 feet. We started climbing all the way to our practice area. When we got there, we were at 2500 feet. He immediately turned the ship over to me, and I did climbing and gliding turns. He said I was doing OK, but I didn't think so. The biggest thrill of the day came when I made one of my climbing turns too steep and he showed me what would happen if I did them too steep. He nosed her up almost to a stall and kicked her into a spin. Golly, what a funny sensation. I was heading straight down toward the earth, and spinning like fury. It was like sitting on something way up high and like some one had started spinning the earth. It sure was fun. Lots of fellows in our flight have gotten sick flying but I didn't get the least bit sick. The only thing I do is look forward to flying every day.

We sure have a tough schedule now. We fly in the morning, have physical training, and then in the afternoon we have Math, Physics and Physics Lab. We have to pick up physics, a whole year of it, in two months, but I'll do anything to get my wings. In my flight, I'm a crew corporal with 9 guys under me. I drill them and march them to class.

They sure are getting strict around here. They give delinquents (gigs) right and left. If you get more than 4, you don't get to have any open post for that week. They give "gigs" mostly on the condition of our room. All of us got gigs the first of the week because there was soap in the sink.

That's sure tough about Keith Ferrell washing out. The further I go along, the greater is the fear that I'll wash out. Well, guess I'd better close now and try to study a little bit.

I'll write as soon as possible. All my love, Cobby

June 9, 1943

Dearest Family,

Well, here it is Wednesday again and I'm almost thru with my flying. I have nine hours dual instruction now, and I have my check flight tomorrow. I hope I can do OK on it. I've improved a lot the last few weeks. I've been getting better grades and I've learned to "feel" the ship. For the past few lessons, I've been doing spins and stalls. Boy, are they fun! I've done a lot of loops, snap rolls, and chandelles. Boy, that is the most exciting sensation in the world. It makes a roly coaster seem so simple. I love to fly more than anything. It seems like you're all alone in the world, and it's so beautiful flying, then the instructor starts giving you hell for something done wrong. All my love, Cobby

Cobby's eight-week training at Transylvania ended, and he was given a taste of flying an airplane, discipline to be a good soldier, and academic instruction in math and physics. His next stop was in Nashville, Tennessee, for three months at the AAF Southeast Classification Pre-Flight Training Center. There he received his indoctrination into military life—the GI haircut, inoculations, guard duty, and the infamous K.P. (Kitchen Patrol). Cobby underwent rigid medical exams and numerous types of aptitude and physical tests.

Cobby looked to Nashville as just another stop in his journey to become a pilot. Little did he know that his life would change forever in those two short months.

REFERENCES

[1] "AAF Training During WWII." National Museum of the USAF. Accessed May 15, 2012. http://www.nationalmuseum.af.mil/factsheets/factsheet.asp?id=1675.

[2] *U.S. Army Aviation Cadets, Keep'em Flying (1942)*. Pamphlet. U.S. Army Recruiting Service.

3 Ashcroft, B. *We Wanted Wings: A History of the Aviation Cadet Program.* Accessed December 12, 2012. http://www.aetc.af.mil/shared/media/document/AFD-061109-026.pdf

4 "History of Keesler Air Force Base." Keesler Air Force Base. Accessed July 15, 2012. http://www.keesler.af.mil/library/factsheets/factsheet.asp?id=4881.

5 "About George Marshall." George C. Marshall Foundation on the Internet. Accessed July 15, 2012. http://www.marshallfoundation.org/about/index.html.

CHAPTER FOUR.

Finding Love in Nashville, June 1943

Cobby arrived in Nashville, Tennessee, in June, when the air was very humid and the weather was uncomfortably hot. He would spend the next nine weeks following orders and doing guard duty and kitchen patrol, while taking aptitude and physical tests to determine whether he was best suited for training as a pilot, navigator, or bombardier. Once his classification was determined, he would enter preflight ground school.

This Southern town of 250,000 residents was flooded with soldiers, including aviation cadets arriving daily on trains to process through the southeastern region classification center. Aviation training programs for the B-17 Flying Fortress and B-24 Liberators were at nearby air bases, and hundreds of those planes flying in formation would fill the skies over Nashville. In addition, Middle Tennessee was a major training site for Army soldiers because of the similarity between the rural countryside and the terrain of western Europe. Tennessee Maneuvers would train over 800,000 Army soldiers over a four-year period, and these divisions would later be part of major battles in Normandy and Belgium, including the Battle of the Bulge.

The weekends in Nashville were overflowing with thousands of young men seeking recreational activities. Popular options included going to movies, but many soldiers visited local bars and brothels, and the latter combination created health and legal problems for all involved. The need for other weekend recreational activities to support servicemen in their off-duty hours prompted the YMCA and United Service Organization (USO) to organize dances on Saturday nights. These events included a live band with USO junior hostess volunteers who socialized and danced with the soldiers. Snacks and non-alcoholic beverages were served, and many soldiers took advantage of this opportunity on Saturday nights.

Cobby went to a YMCA dance where he fell hard and fast for a lovely volunteer named Evelyn. He spent as much time as possible with her over the next few weeks, and this magical connection formed a foundation for an enduring love sustained through letters in the coming months and years.

June 23, 1943

Dearest Family,

I'm writing this letter from Nashville, Tennessee. We got here Sunday about 9:00, and they've had us working ever since. I tried to call you but we're quarantined for two weeks, and I can't get to a phone. This camp is a lot better than Keesler Field, but boy, is it hot. I haven't perspired so much in all my life, and the water we drink is hot.

We left Lexington Saturday about 4:30 and got here around 9:00. Boy, the cars we had were modified cattle cars and were hot and uncomfortable. I was placed in charge of the whole group coming down and what a headache that was, seeing that the fellows didn't tear up the car and raise hell in general. From what I can gather, we'll be here 4 or 5 weeks. It will take about two weeks for our classification and then we have K.P. and guard duty every other day.

Boy, you should see the planes flying around down here. They are mostly B-24 (Liberators) but today I saw five P-38's (Lockheed Lightnings) fly over in formation. All my love, Cobby

The B-24 Liberator

Courtesy of National Museum of the U.S. Air Force
"These planes literally fill up the sky!" [Cobby Webb]

The B-24 is a heavy bomber and a real threat to the enemy with a crew of 10 men, four movable machine guns, and 8,000 lbs. of bombs. This plane flew more missions and dropped more bombs than any other aircraft in the war.

The Lockheed P-38

Courtesy of National Museum of the U.S. Air Force
"This is my kind of plane!" [Cobby Webb]

The P-38 is a fast plane and long-range escort fighter that can also be used for dive bombing, level bombing, and ground strafing. The Germans call it "the forked-tailed devil."

The Boeing B-17 Flying Fortress

Courtesy of National Museum of the U.S. Air Force
"A Flying Tank" [Cobby Webb]

The B-17 is a gigantic multi-engine effective bomber that was built to fly high and fast. It is equipped with swinging machine guns to fight oncoming fighter planes and a precise targeting system for bomb drops. The "Flying Fortress" is also legendary for its ability to stay in the air after taking brutal poundings.

June 28, 1943

Dearest Family,
I've been pretty busy here getting settled. I took 8 hours of mental exams yesterday and tomorrow I take the psycho-motor exams. They say those are a lot of fun, just like a penny arcade.

Boy, is it hot and dusty here! Whew! I'm sweating like mad and it's pretty cool this morning. I guess you know that we're quarantined here for two weeks. No open post or anything, we don't even get out of the area. I'll sure be glad when I finish my classification and get shipped to pre-flight someplace. I have to take a real tough physical here, and I don't know whether or not my eyes will pass. I'm pretty worried about washing out. I sure hope I don't.

I sure hated to leave ol' Transy. That was a life of leisure. I wish I wasn't so smart, and that I was in A flight, then maybe I could get home again. I've been trying like the devil to figure something out so I can get home. If I can hit a loophole and get a pass for a few days, you can bet your bottom dollar I'll be home with bells on. Give everyone at home my regards. All my love, Cobby

July 6, 1943

Dearest Family,

I'm sure sorry that I haven't written, but you know how things slip by. I just got off K.P. about ½ hour ago and boy did I work hard today. I haven't received my classification yet, but I think I'm a hot pilot. I'm not sure but I'll probably know tomorrow.

I'm sending some money home in this letter. It's quite a pile. I've been using some gallopin' dominoes on the boys that talk to me like a brother. I'm practically worth my weight in gold.

Did I tell you about me trying my best to dodge work? Well, I was doing a darn good job of it up until today, and they snagged me for K.P., and that put an end to all of my loafing, but they'll never catch me again, though, because I know how to loaf and get away with it now.

I've had two open posts since I've been here of 5 hours each and I went into Nashville. Oh, what a lousy town it is, so many soldiers it's pitiful.

This army life is teaching me how to appreciate my home and family. When I get back from the war, we'll get us a big house and get all of us Webbs up there, and we'll all raise a big family. I mean Clayton's and my kids. Write soon and often. All my love, Cobby

P.S. I got the cake and cookies. The cake was all mashed to hell, but the cookies were in fine shape.

They both were very good, only I wouldn't advise sending anymore cakes through the mail.

July 13, 1943

Dearest Family,

Well, here I am on guard duty again. It seems I'm always doing something anymore. Boy, is it hot down here.

Hey Pop, I got your letter today, and you sounded as though you had me in the dog house for winning all that dough. Well, don't forget you always told me never to gamble unless I could afford to lose. Well, I thought I could afford to lose, but won. I haven't shot any craps since then. Don't worry about me losing all my jack, 'cause I set aside a certain amount to lose—if I lose that, I quit. It just so happened that I got lucky and won. I understand the chances of losing, so don't worry about me. Whether you realize it or not, I'm becoming a man.

Give my regards to everyone. Love, Cobby

July 19, 1943

Dearest Family,

Well, I've been here four weeks now and the past two have been terrible. I just got off guard duty a few minutes ago and I'm now in my barracks. It seems as though I don't do anything but work anymore and you know how I hate work. This makes the second guard duty I've had in the past week, and besides that, I was on maintenance day before yesterday.

When we had open post Wednesday, one of my
buddies and myself went to a Cadet dance at the
Y.M.C.A. and met a couple of broads there. They were
pretty nice, so we made dates for Friday and went to
the Commodore Room in the Andrew Jackson Hotel.
They musta liked us pretty much 'cause they called up
our Squadron tactical officer and invited us to their
homes for Saturday evening, but we had guard duty
and they wouldn't let us off. Boy, am I burned up
about it.

There are 200 in our squadron and about 40 or 50
more guys will wash out before we finish our training.
I have my fingers crossed. Well, I guess I better go now.
All my love, Cobby

Evelyn Groves is an attractive, petite, eighteen-year-old woman with
chestnut brown, wavy hair, soft hazel eyes, and a big smile that lights up her
face. She is cheerful and intuitive, and people are drawn to her fun-loving
nature and sweet personality. Evelyn lives with her mother and stepfather
in a middle-income, downtown neighborhood on the east side of the
city, within walking distance of the school and bus stop. She maintains
an optimistic view of life, although her life has not always been easy. Her
parents divorced when she was five years old, and her biological father left
the state, taking her eight-year-old brother, Neil, with him. In those days,
divorce was not about joint custody, it was about separation, and Evelyn has
not seen Neil since that day. Her mother remarried a kind man who is the
father she needs, but Evelyn misses the relationship with her brother. That
loss is not discussed, but accepted, and Evelyn learned at an early age to live
in the moment because life is unpredictable.

In 1943 Evelyn is beginning her adult life in the workforce following
high school. It is an unsettled world that is rapidly changing and an
environment filled with worry and anxiety as good friends, classmates, and
neighbors are leaving for the war, and some will not return home.

Reminders of war are all around, as the quiet town of Nashville is
exploding with men in uniform on every street corner and you could hear
the rumble of war planes flying overhead across the sky. Evelyn found
routine and normalcy in her life through her job at the National Life and

Accident Insurance Company, volunteering with the Red Cross, and socializing with her girlfriends. At a friend's request, Evelyn volunteered to be a junior hostess on Saturday nights at the USO-sponsored dances held at the YMCA. She considered it an opportunity to dance and have a good time while visiting with soldiers stationed temporarily in Nashville. The dances are held in a large ballroom area where an orchestra plays those favorite songs from the swing era, and hundreds of men in uniform are dancing or milling around in the adjoining room where refreshments are served, while others are gathered in small groups of conversation. Cobby wandered into the YMCA one Saturday night with several buddies from the base, and it didn't take long for him to notice Evelyn. He asked her to dance, and they ended up on the dance floor together all evening. Their attraction to one another was spontaneous and immediate, and after a few weeks of dating, Cobby is convinced he has found his soul mate and future wife. In fact, he told her on their second date that he planned to marry her, and they would spend the next year getting to know each other through letters.

"My Evaline"

July 25, 1943

Dearest Family,

Well, another week has gone by already, and we're about ready to ship. I think Tuesday. I had three swell dates with the gal I was telling you about. Evelyn Groves is her name. I was out at her house last night and we ate a whole freezer of homemade ice cream. Man! Was it good!

Golly Dad, I'm sure bitter at the army and the p-poor officers who represent it tonite. You know Evelyn's mother called up our C.O. and asked him to let me come out to her house this evening for a picnic. Well, he was going to give me a pass until right after the parade this morning, when I went to mail call to pick up a package (here comes the bitter part). In my excitement I went over without my hat to the Day Room to get my package and on the way back to the barracks, a distance of about 100 feet, a captain stopped me and asked where my hat was. I told him it was in the barracks. So he asked my name and about five minutes later the C.O. called me in and gave me holy hell, and took my pass away for tonite, just because I'd forgotten my hat. Can you beat that? Those _____well, I won't say it. You know, Pop, if I'm around here much longer I'm going to be court-martialed, 'cause I can't take much more of this "crap" they're handing me around here. I'm afraid I'll poke one of these 90-day wonders. Up until two weeks ago, I didn't mind the army, but since then I'm building up a hatred for some of these officers who sling unreasonable orders, and who aren't half as good as me. I'm just about at the end of my rope. I'm sorry this letter is so gripy, but I had to get this off my chest. Write me soon. All my love, Cobby

P.S. Tell Clayton not to take his hurt shoulder so hard, he'll be OK soon. Tell him to keep his chin up, like you tell me to.

July 31, 1943

Dearest Family,

I'm sorry that I haven't written before, but this letter is kinda hard for me to write, and I've been neglecting it, like you neglect all unpleasant things. Of course, Pop, you know that I missed shipment, but you don't know why. Well, to get right down to brass tacks, the day we were going to ship, we didn't have anything to do, so a little crap game was started. I immediately got into it, for amusement only. Well, as it turned out, it was my unlucky day because we were caught. So here I am. I am held back for punishment only. Now when you answer this letter, don't say "I told you so." I knew it was wrong and I'll take what's coming to me. But believe you me I've learned my lesson. That hard headedness of mine cropping out again. I guess I'll always have to learn the hard way. But where I fooled 'em is, I don't mind staying here, because I have a little business in Nashville that requires the utmost consideration and contemplation! Yep! It's a she, and what a gal. She understands me—get that! We like the same things and really get along swell. Sunday I went out to her house and ate fried chicken until I thought I was going to start cackling. When you all come down, you'll have the pleasure of meeting her.

I'll write and tell you definitely when I'm going to be leaving, but I'll have to find out first. I'm fairly sure it will be four or five weeks. All my love! Cobby

P.S. Don't worry about me too much. I'm gradually learning I'm in the army.

P.S. I'm now Squadron Commander over 19 navigators, 4 pilots, 1 bombardier, 5 washouts and 8 men in the hospital. We haven't done anything but putter around, so I'm having a luxurious time here.

August 12, 1943

Dearest Family,

I'm sure sorry that I haven't written before now but I've been terribly busy these last few days getting the squadron organized and keeping these rookies on the ball. Say, how is everyone back in ol' St. Albans? I mean the ones who are still left there.

I've just finished calling good old St. Albans. I sure was glad to hear your voice, Mom, but sure was disappointed I didn't get to talk to you, Pop. Mom, you don't think I'm crazy, do you? I'll tell ya, this little gal down here is so wonderful, she's just about the sweetest thing I've ever met. She really sends me. Just wait until you meet Evelyn, mom, then you'll know that your baby is in good hands. I've never felt like this about any girl before and I've had lots of gals in my life. Even you all know that. When I put my arms around her I go completely "out of this world!!" Hey! My golly, what am I saying? I believe I'm just a big softy. I gotta quit saying things like that or people will think I'm a sissy. Gotta go now. All my love, Cobby

August 27, 1943

Dearest Family,

Well, I'm finally getting ready to ship out and we're restricted to the post. Boy, are they getting tough around here. They caught about 30 guys out on somebody else's passes so they washed them out, court-martialed them and took 2/3 of their pay!

Evelyn and I had dinner last night and afterwards a movie. I think she's the sweetest girl I've ever known and if she'll have me I'd like to marry her. I'm sitting here in the telephone office waiting on a phone to call Evelyn and I do believe I'm sorta getting blue. Golly Dad, I sure hate to leave ol' Evelyn. She's the gal for me.

Has Clayton gone out for football yet? Tell him to give everything he's got and not to piddle around or he's liable to get hurt.

I'll sure be glad when I get to my pre-flight school. I'm pretty sure it will be Maxwell but you never can tell. I may be sent further west. Give my regards to everyone, and tell 'em I'll be seeing 'em. All my love, Cobby

REFERENCES

1   "Initial Selection of Candidates for Pilot, Bombardier, and Navigator Training." Army Air Forces Historical Studies, Prepared by Assistant Chief of Air Staff Intelligence Historical Division. Accessed August 15, 2012. http://www.afhra.af.mil/shared/media/document/AFD-090602-023.pdf.

2   Cravens, W.F., Ed. *The Army Air Forces in World War II Vol. VI: Men and Planes*. Accessed August 20, 2012. http://www.ibiblio.org/hyperwar/AAF/VI/AAF-VI-17.html

3   "Tennessee 4 Me, WWII, Working for the War: Military Bases in Tennessee." Tennessee State Museum. Accessed July 10, 2012. http://www.tn4me.org/article.cfm/a_id/220/minor_id/72/major_id/9/era_id/7.

4   McMillin, W. *In the Presence of Soldiers: The 2nd Army Maneuvers and Other World War II Activity in Tennessee*. Nashville: 830 Summerly Drive, Nashville TN 37209.

5   Winchell, M.K. *Good Girls, Good Food, Good Fun: The Story of USO Hostesses During World War II*. Chapel Hill: The University of North Carolina Press.

6   Consolidated B-24 Liberator Fact Sheet and Photo. The Official Website of National Museum of the USAF. Accessed May 15, 2011. http://www.nationalmuseum.af.mil/factsheets/factsheet.asp?id=494.

7   Lockheed P-38 Fact Sheet and Photo. The Official Website of National Museum of the USAF. Accessed May 15, 2011. http://www.

nationalmuseum.af.mil/factsheets/ factsheet.asp?id=2201, and http://www. nationalmuseum.af.mil/shared/media/ photodb/photos/061019-F-1234P-011.jpg.

8   Boeing B-17 G Flying Fortress Fact Sheet and Photo. The Official Website of National Museum of the USAF. Accessed May 15, 2011. http://www. nationalmuseum.af.mil/factsheets/ factsheet.asp?id=512.

CHAPTER FIVE

Preflight Training, September 1943

Cobby was shipped out to Maxwell Field in Alabama, the Southeast Air Corps Training Center, for preflight training, where he received more instruction in mathematics and sciences as related to the mechanics and physics of flight, as well as intensive physical training. "In the morning we take 2 hours of aircraft identification, Morse code and an hour of Math," Cobby wrote. "In the afternoon we have military sanitation, physical training and drill." The aircraft identification involved flash cards with silhouettes flashed on a screen at 1/10 of a second so the men could learn and distinguish the different types of American, British, German, and Japanese planes so that targeting our own aircraft during combat could be avoided.

The Maxwell Air Corps Training Center ran pilot, navigator, and bombardier training for over 100,000 aviation cadets during World War II. Women also played an important role at Maxwell Field during the war. In 1943, over 150 members of the Women's Army Auxiliary Corps (WAAC) came to Maxwell to work as clerks, technicians, stenographers, radio and telephone operators, to free up men for combat duty. In 1941, the United States set up a pilot training program at several training sites, including Maxwell, where British cadets would receive instruction to qualify for combat in the Royal Air Force. From 1941 to 1943, over four thousand Britons graduated from pilot training in the United States.

August 31, 1943

Maxwell Field, Alabama

Dearest Family,
 I'm now at Maxwell Field, a beautiful place for permanent party men, but for cadets it's no good. The upper classmen really make you hump. Do this, do that, don't do this! etc. Yes indeed, I'm right disgusted with Maxwell Field. I sure wish I was back in Nashville leading a life of luxury.

We left Nashville Sunday night at 7:30 and arrived in Montgomery at 5:00 in the morning, where we were met by Cadet Officers with sabers on, who acted like they owned the world, and that you were just another ant to be stepped on.

I've seen all of my buddies who came down last month and they seem very happy. I guess it will be OK in a couple of days. My buddies will be leaving here in about 4 weeks to go to a primary school. In two weeks we'll get our first open post and after four weeks, when we're made upperclassmen, we'll get every other week-end off for 27 hours. Well, I guess I'd better go, they're calling us out for something. All my love, Cobby.

September 8, 1943

Dearest Family,

We started classes Thursday, and boy, are they a pain. We get up at 4:30 A.M. and our first class starts at 6:00 A.M., and I used to gripe about 8 o'clocks back at Miami. We are taking two hours of aircraft identification, an hour of code and an hour of math. That code is really tough and I'm really having to struggle with it. We have these classes in the morning, and during the afternoon we have Military Sanitation and Physical Training and Drill. The physical training down here is really tough. Yesterday, we ran the "Burma road," a cross country trail full of pot holes and natural pitfalls. Several guys have suffered serious injuries and a couple have died of heat exhaustion this summer.

We had our first Saturday Morning Inspection today, and we started cleaning our room last night. We passed OK, but I think it was by the Grace of God.

Right now we're listening to the "Hit Parade" that is playing over the P.A. system, and Frankie has the women in the studio audience screaming and sighing like mad. Our barrack is right next door to the Cadet Recreation Hall, and they have a wonderful dance floor right outside our window, and every night they have a dance I lay in the bed listening to the music, and I get so damn blue. I think of Evelyn and home and all the swell times I used to have. I sure wish this war would end!

Well, I guess I'd better go for now. I gotta wash yet and get ready for bed. It's almost 9:00 and that's the time the taps blow for us. I'm pretty tired at the end of the day because we're on the go about 14 hours a day. We have study period from 7 till 8:30 every night and that's when I usually write my letters. I started this one this morning and I'm just finishing now so that can give you some idea how we're rushed. Write soon. All my love, Cobby

September 10, 1943

Dearest Family,

I just got my watch and the candy—thanks a lot! I got a card from Evelyn's mother telling me that Evelyn was in the hospital with appendicitis and had an operation. Why don't you all drop her a letter or card in care of St. Thomas Hospital in Nashville?

I'm getting to like this place pretty well now. The time goes pretty fast now that we're going to classes.

So Clayton is out for football? Tell him to stick with it and he'll be a 4-year man which will be quite an accomplishment. I think I know he's big enough and tough enough to be a really good ball player. For goodness sake, Clate, don't be scared of hitting those big guys and knocking the hell out of 'em. Always remember, the harder you hit the other fellow, the easier it's going to be on you. I know you'll be a better player than I ever hoped to be. Just keep in there pluggin' and don't be discouraged if things go wrong once in a while. You have a wonderful talent for athletics, develop it and take care of it.

Say, it's really too bad about Herman Stevens, missing in action. Has it been confirmed? If not, maybe he's OK. Well, I'd better close for now. Be sure and write soon. All my love, Cobby

Little did Cobby know that his fourteen-year-old old brother, Clayton Webb, would three years later be selected as the number one high school football player in West Virginia. Clayton would receive a football scholarship to the University of Kentucky, where he would play under Coach Paul "Bear" Bryant. During his college career, Clayton would be selected for the 1951 All-SEC team and drafted by the Pittsburg Steelers.

Cobby makes many references to Clayton and football throughout his letters.

September 14, 1943

Dearest Family,

I've been sleeping most of the day, 'cause I'm really tired after 6 days of classes around here. You have to sleep all day Sunday so you'll be ready for the next week. I've had a couple of exams already, one in Aircraft Identification, which I got a 90 on and one in Math. I racked outa 95 but I'm disgusted with myself 'cause I didn't make a hundred. I should have because it's very elementary. The only thing I'm having trouble with is code.

For the last several days we've been getting lectures on the high altitude chamber. I guess we'll get it tomorrow or the next day, then they take us up to 18,000 feet without oxygen, then they take us up to 38,000 feet with oxygen masks. They say that's quite an experience.

We had two parades this week, one for General Welsh, and they gave him an 11-gun, I mean cannon, salute. It was a pretty impressive affair even though I didn't enjoy marching out in the hot sun.

Well, our whole squadron and class of 44E are mad enough to chew nails. We've just been informed, much to our chagrin, that we won't get open post for 3 more weeks! Now ain't that a bunch of bull?

Did you all write Evelyn? I think she needs cheering up more than me. Write soon. All my love,
Cobby

September 23, 1943

Dearest Family,

It won't be long until we'll be upper classmen, probably a week from today. The other class is leaving next Wednesday for their primary schools and then we'll be upper classmen. They say about 30% are washing out of primary and that's pretty high for some of 'em. I think that maybe my chances are getting a little better of making it.

I'm sure glad you all wrote Evelyn. She sure is a swell gal and the letters will help cheer her up. I hear from her almost every day and everything is still perkin' 'tween us.

About that insurance, that's what the govt. is giving me. Instead of me paying for it anymore, being I'm now a cadet, I get it for nothing.

Tell ol' Clayton to keep pluggin' for the football team, tell 'im Rome wasn't built in a day and that as soon as he learns a little more about taking care of himself in a game he'll be playing first string.

We had the High Altitude Chamber Monday night, and what a funny experience. We only went to 5,000 feet first, then we came down and then went to 30,000 feet for an hour and then 38,000 feet for 15 minutes. We wore oxygen masks and breathed pure oxygen from 10,000 feet on up. It was kinda fun I thought, but of course I didn't have any trouble with my sinus or ears, but some of the fellows had terrific pains in their ears, and some almost ruptured an ear drum. I was sorta scared of the pressure chamber, but now I know I'm OK for high altitude flying. Well, I gotta go now and start cleaning up. We're having a big stand-by inspection by the Commandant of Cadets tomorrow and we have a lot of work to do. Write soon and often. All my love, Cobby

September 29, 1943

Dearest Family,

How's Mom gettin' along with her teachin' the little kids? Has she paddled anyone yet? How do you like doing housework "Pop?" Ha! I gotta big kick outta your letter, when you said you'd just finished your breakfast dishes and sweeping the back porch.

Well, the class ahead of us leaves this week-end, and all of them are hepped up about it as well as us, who will become upper classmen when they leave. We had a couple of final exams today, one in Math and one in Aircraft Identification. Incidentally, I racked 100% on the Math, but it is so simple it bores me, but Aircraft Identification is another story. I'll consider myself lucky to have passed that. We had 45 planes flashed on the screen at 1/10 of a second and we had to give the name and wingspan of each plane. It's pretty rugged!

We had open post Friday night and Sunday, but I have to stay in 'cause I got a few demerits last week for this and that. Nothin' serious. Everybody walks tours around here, so don't worry!!

We have guard duty tonight, on the flight line. We guard all the planes on the field. I'm on from 0200 till 0400, so I'll get to see a lotta "liberators" shooting night landings. We carry rifles and supposedly live ammunition. But I'm disgusted with the whole deal. I thought I was getting away from this dern guard duty when I left Nashville! But we're only on two hours as it is, so it won't be too bad.

Hey Clate, how are you getting along with that old feetball? Now don't be gettin' discouraged because you aren't playing first string. You're inexperienced this year, but boy! Wait'll next year! So boy, keep pluggin' and don't let up and you'll be a big star.

Well, I went to church today, but only because it was compulsory. All in all it was a good sermon and it was pretty interesting. I'll send you the program. Be sure you all write me lots! All my love, Cobby

P.S. Evelyn is OK and she sent her regards via "Cobweb." She hasn't gone back to work yet, but is rapidly recovering.

The above-mentioned church program was still enclosed with the letter. The following prayer, a petition for safety, honored the young men, our country's sons, who would be sacrificing health and life in the pursuit of peace. A somber tribute.

PROTESTANT CHURCH SERVICES
Maxwell Field, Alabama
September 26, 1943
FOR THESE OUR SONS

O Lord of Life, Strength of the strong, and best Guide of our youth: the anguish of a nation's strong fatherhood and the tears of its sacrificing motherhood prompt our prayer for the lads of our land. They are leaving our homes and altars to heed their country's call. They are shouldering arms, flying planes and manning ships in defense of the flag. Here in the friendly pew and at the family altar we follow them in dusty march, airy flight and stormy sea with our petitions for safety. May their remoteness from sanctuary and home not lessen their grip on the virtues of a royal manhood. These are our sons. Thy choice gift to us, and our heart's desire is that they may serve our country's cause unsullied and unstained. Above all, dear Lord, guide them by Thy Holy Spirit that they may keep sacred in the crowded routine of each day some fraction of time for a prayer tryst with Thee. And our heart's plea, O Father of all the nations of the earth, is that enduring peace may soon come to supplant the sword, hate giving way to love, and brutality to brotherhood. In the Name of our Elder Brother, the Prince of Peace. (John F. Fedders)

October 7, 1943

Dearest Family,

Well, only two more days till Open Post. I'll sure appreciate O.P. this week because we've really been on the go all week. For the last couple of days, we've been going to gunnery school and learning all about the .45, and we went to the range Monday morning. That afternoon, we had 5 classes, the same thing Wednesday. On Tuesday, we had P.T. in the morning, also gunnery school, 3 classes in the afternoon, plus two hours of drill. So far I've been doing pretty good in my studies but it's not because I'm brilliant. The stuff we have is so simple my academic average is 93%. I wish I could do just as well in civilian life.

We eat two meals per day in the dark, breakfast and dinner. Breakfast at 0600 and dinner at 1900. I like that 'cause you don't have to polish shoes or brass when you can't see 'em. The food down here is terrible. We're on field rations and we don't get enough to eat, and what we do get is no darn good.

The latest latrinogram is that we'll go to Arcadia, Florida, where, when you have soloed, they put 7 days rations and a .45 automatic in your plane, because you spend most of your time flying over the everglades.

Well, we have a little drill session coming up so I'll close. All my love, Cobby

October 28, 1943

Dearest Family,

Sorry I'm late on this letter, but I have a cold and I don't feel like doing anything but lying around.

It's cold as the very devil and we're wearing our overcoats. We drill all the free time we have and everyone in the squadron is griping like mad. We leave for primary on Wed., Nov. 3 for the flying field I least wanted to go to—Arcadia, Florida. They say it's pretty rough down there. Well, there's nothing that can be done about it. One good thing is that they have brand new Stearman P.T. 17's there, one consolation anyhow.

Did I tell you all that Evelyn isn't going to get to come down for the final dance, and after I had planned so much on her coming down? Sure am disappointed about Evelyn. How's everything with you all?

Today the awards were given out and our squadron won the cup as the best squadron in the group. Well, I gotta go now. By the time you get this letter I'll have reached my destination. Sorry I couldn't call, I'll try to from Fla. All my love, Cobby

REFERENCES

[1] "Maxwell Air Force Base, Alabama." The Military Standard-Air Force Bases. Accessed May 30, 2012. http://www.techbastard.com/afb/al/maxwell.php.

CHAPTER SIX

Into the Sky, November 1943

The next phase of Cobby's pilot training was eight weeks at Carlstrom Field in Arcadia, Florida, for Primary Flying School. Here, he learned the fundamentals of flying in a two-seater aircraft and completed sixty hours of flight training. The flight instructors for primary flying schools were civilian pilots under contract with the government because there were so many aviation cadets going through training and not enough military instructors. While at Carlstrom Field, Cobby spent his first Thanksgiving and Christmas holidays away from home.

November 6, 1943

Arcadia, Florida

Dearest Family,
Well, I'm now starting the phase of my training that I've waited 8½ months for. We arrived here yesterday afternoon around 2:00 and got settled. We were issued our books and our flying equipment today. So I guess we'll start right in flying. We have our first classes tomorrow. We have twelve subjects, from Theory of Flight to Structure of Airplanes with Navigation and a host of others thrown in.
I'm very well satisfied with my new home. The barracks are terrific, very beautiful, with tennis courts and a swimming pool. There are palm trees all around the place and the grass is very green and beautiful, like a beautiful lawn. There are four of us in a room and I'm rooming with three of the fellows I roomed with at Maxwell Field. The rooms are very large with a private shower and toilette in each room. The food here isn't too good, but it's better than the food at Maxwell.

The trip down here was very enjoyable, the food was good, and the trip seemed short even though we were on the train about 30 hours. They have 150 Stearman P.T. 17's, and the sky is filled with them all of the time.

Things are going along swell around here—only one thing I don't like is the water. We have sulphur water, and it is terrible. Well, I gotta go to an orientation lecture, so until next letter, all my love, Cobby

Stearman PT-17

Courtesy of National Museum of the U.S. Air Force
"The PT-17's here are new and I can't wait to start flying!" [Cobby Webb]

The Stearman PT-17 is a standard biplane primary trainer flown by aviation cadets in World War II.

November 9, 1943

Dearest Family,

Guess what? I'm now a veteran of the air with a grand total of 58 minutes, gained this afternoon! It was really terrific! We have more homework to do. I've taken notes in class and on the flight line until I am blue in the face. The classes are very interesting. We have two classes a day now—Theory of Flight, where we learn how an airplane flies and why. Then a class on aircraft engines and now I know the difference in a connecting rod and a rocker arm—it's really great stuff. We're still drilling on Aircraft Identification, now at 1/25 of a second and it's really fast. If you blink an eye you miss it.

Now for surprise, guess what I did yesterday? Well, first I got up at 0800, had breakfast, went to a couple of classes, had lunch, now the good part, I played tennis all afternoon, and got a nice tan, then I took a cool refreshing dip in the pool, all of which took place on November 7. Ah, it's a great life and you can't beat it. This is the part of the Air Corps they put on enlistment posters.

Well, I gotta go take a hike. We have a big G.I. movie to occupy us when we really need the time to study. Write soon. All my love, Cobby

November 15, 1943

Dearest Family,

Here it is Sunday and I've been flying for a week. It is really great! I have 5 hours and 41 minutes flying time and I expect to solo sometime next week if nothing happens. The instructor I have really raises hell with us when we don't do something right, but he knows his stuff and can really pound the business of flying into our thick skulls.

For the last two days I've been practicing landings and takeoffs, and between you n' me, I haven't made a three pointer yet without something being wrong but I'm learning and I'll have it down pat in a couple more flying hours. My takeoffs are good, but they're easy. And my coordination is fair. All in all I guess I'm just about an average student. Nothin' extra.

How's everyone back home? I'm fine. I'm in swell shape, really have a fine physical edge, no fat, all muscle, and I'm down to 170. But this flying is really a mental strain and I'm dog tired every night. The physical training is pretty tough, too, but I feel good after doing it.

There's a P-47 Transition school around here and they buzz the field all the time. I looked over a P-47 close the other day, and they are huge with a maze of instruments. Can't give you any particulars, but they carry 4-50's in each wing plus cannon in nose. Really a terrific ship.

Haven't heard from Evelyn yet. She must be pretty busy. Give my regards to all. All my love, Cobby

Republic P-47 D Thunderbolt

Courtesy of National Museum of the U.S. Air Force
"The P-47 is really a terrific ship." [Cobby Webb]

This plane is known for its toughness, firepower, and speed and is one of the most important USAAF fighters in World War II. The P-47, nicknamed "Thunderbolt" is a rugged airplane that served as a high-altitude escort fighter and a low-level fighter-bomber. During World War II, the P-47 served in almost every active war theatre and in the air forces of several Allied nations.

Turkey Day, 1943

Dearest Family,
     Here I am in class on TURKEY DAY of all days. I thought they'd give us a half day off, but no such luck, classes in the morning and flying in the afternoon. I have 15 hours flying time now, and about 4 hours of it is solo. I'm really having a pretty tough time. I can do the spins and stalls OK but I'll be durned if I can get the simpler maneuvers, like "S" turns across the road and elementary eights. I'll probably get my 20 hour check the first of next week. I'm already beginning to worry. They've already washed about 15 guys out of my class, before they ever soloed.

The weather here is very nice, not hot and not cold, but just right. I have to fly in overalls and a leather jacket and I never get cold even up to 5,000 feet. Day before yesterday I climbed to 5,000 ft and was doing spins, by myself, and I decided to get down in a hurry. So I spun to 2500 ft, leveled off and glided to 550 ft fast to enter traffic pattern to land. Well, when I hit 550 ft, I thought my head was going to blow right off. My eyes started watering and my nose was running like mad. At first I thought I'd had a hemorrhage due to change of altitude, but there wasn't any blood, so I finally realized when I got on the ground that I had a cold and my sinuses were draining, causing all the pain, and after that I didn't have a cold anymore. So if you have a head cold sometime, go up to 5000 feet and come down in a hurry. I'll guarantee that you won't have a cold when you get on the ground.

I have received all the packages and got the one you sent for Thanksgiving. Well, here's wishing you a Happy Thanksgiving. All my love, Cobby

December 1, 1943

Dearest Family,

I know, I know, I'm late but there is a good reason! I've really been busy these last few days. I now have 20 hours flying time and my 20-hour check is due any day. Boy, I'm sorta worried about that 20-hour check I have coming up. I sure hope everything goes OK. Keep your fingers crossed. I'll probably have had the check by the time this letter gets to you all.

Today a couple of guys in my group got lost. The weather was pretty bad for flying anyhow. At 1500 ft the ground haze was so bad you could hardly see the ground. I almost got lost myself. Well, anyhow this kid got lost and flew down to Ft. Myers about 50 or 60 miles from here. When he landed down there among the B-17's and B-26's, he was scared to death. He walked into the operational tower and asked them where the hell he was. They took one look at him and at the PT-17 he was flying, laughed and said Alaska, and razzed him something terrific. He called the field and they sent an instructor down after him in an AT-6 and brought him and his plane back.

I hope you are all well and happy. I'm fine both in spirit and body. Give all my love to everyone. All my love, Cobby

P.S. Mom I'm flying PT-17's, not B-17's!!!!!!!

December 6, 1943

Dearest Family,

Well, another rest day is at an end and I feel fresh for my next week's flying. Oh by the way, I had my 20-hour check Friday, and I passed, by the grace of God, 'cause I think I flew worse that day than I have yet. Guess who I had to ride??? Major Clouts, the Post Commander. Boy, you think I wasn't scared. I was so excited that when he kicked me into an unexpected accidental spin, I forgot to cut the throttle, and when I pulled out of it I was doing about 160 m.p.h. straight at terra firma, and when I brought the nose up I thought the ship was going to lose its wings, and ol' Cobweb was going to gain a set, but the ol' ship stayed in one piece. I don't guess anything will hurt 'em.

I sure have been having fun flying by myself. I've been doing loops and even "buzzed" a flock of geese the other day. I did a loop and when I got to the top I cut my throttle and rode along upside down. What a thrill, that old safety belt cuttin' into your legs, and you're hanging on to the stick for dear life, and you can't get your feet to touch the rudder petals.

Boy, a lotta guys are washing out now. I think one of my roommates is getting the ax Monday. He's feeling pretty low about now.

I got all the packages you sent for Thanksgiving and also underwear & cookies. Yep Mother, I need dress shoes and also some sweat socks. See what Santa can do.

Yesterday I sent you all a crate of oranges C.O.D. I'm sorry and I hate to say anything about this, but I'm flat broke. Could you advance me a little money till payday? Thanks!

Well, I hate to close asking for money but you know how it is (I hope). Write soon. All my love, Cobby

December 21, 1943

Dearest Family,

Sorry I missed writing yesterday but a buddy and I went to Sarasota for the week-end. I had my 40-hour check the other day and I passed with flying colors. In about two more weeks the 60-hour checks will be coming up and then off to basics. That will be around the 6th or 7th of January and after I get settled, I'll expect you for a visit. Evelyn said she might come down in January, too, so maybe you all can get together and come down at the same time. The weather here is beautiful, nice and warm, bright sunshiny days, and the nights are wonderful. What a place for romance—big bright stars, and last night a huge yellow moon.

I had a cross country flight today, dual, lotta fun but sorta monotonous. I'm at the acrobatic stage now, slow rolls, snap rolls, loops, chandelles, everything. More fun.

Write soon. All my love, Cobby

December 27, 1943

Dearest Family,
    I hope you all had as good a Christmas as I did.
You all really shouldn't have spent so much money.
Boy Dad, thanks a lot for the radio. I've always wanted
a portable. I'm listening to it now. I have the Fitch
Bandwagon [Dixieland brass boogie band] on now.
There are always some guys down listening to the
jive, and it sure brings a lot of enjoyment to all of us.
Thanks again, Pop. Mom, I don't know how you did it,
but that toilet kit is really useful, I've used it already
and add that to my new shoes, I'm really fixed up. And
with that scarf you sent, Clate, I'll really look like the
hot pilot I am with that on and streaming out behind
me in the slipstream. I just can't put down on paper
the thanks I want to give you all for everything. I gotta
a cake from Aunt Cora, cigarettes from Aunt Mary,
wool socks and cigs from Uncle Gene, cigs and socks
from Aleen & Uncle JV and a big picture of Ev, and
cigs from Evelyn. Believe you me, I am really smoking
up a storm.
    I had a good Christmas but it wasn't complete
without you all. It was an ordeal I hope to never
repeat. I was never more homesick in my life, a couple
of times I damn near broke down and bawled. But I
guess I'm not by myself.
    I have 50 hours to my credit now and it won't
be long until I get my sixty-hour check. That's the
one that's really important 'cause that has to do with
acrobatics. I think I'll do OK though, not braggin' or
anything, but I eat up those rolls, loops and snaps.
The greatest thrill I have is diving to do a loop with a
half roll on top. You have to dive 140 m.p.h. and what
a sensation of speed. I pretend I'm strafing a road
clogged with soldiers and tanks etc. It's more fun!

There are furlough rumors floating around
the post and I must admit some of 'em are very
convincing. All of the basic schools are filled, and the
two classes in them now are way behind in their flying
time because of bad weather. Some of the wise boys say
there won't be any room for us in them. So I'm keeping
my fingers crossed and breathing a prayer that the
brass hats at Headquarters will cut a little red tape and
give all of us lonely K-dets blanket furloughs.

I got your loan, Dad. Thanks a lot. Now I'm
reimbursing you 'cause we got paid Friday.

Well, I gotta go now. Happy New Year and thanks
loads for everything. All my love, Cobby

January 7, 1944

Dearest Family,

I've been pretty busy this week finishing up my
flying. I passed my 65-hour check Tuesday, and after
that I flew 5 hours a day for the next couple of days. I
made a 92 on my Navigation final to breeze thru the
course with a good average. My flying was OK so I'm
not held over. I'm ready for basic, but on account of
bad weather up in Alabama, shipping orders have been
delayed a week. Now we have a week to lounge around
in the Florida sunshine. I'm not gripin' about that.
We're going to basic at Gunter Field, which is located
at Montgomery, Ala. I think that is certain. Now if we
don't have to fly 7 days a week when we get there I'll
be seeing you all in a few weeks. Oh joy! All my love,
Cobby

January 16, 1944

Dearest Family,

Just a note before I leave Carlstrom Field for basic training at Gunter Field, Montgomery, Ala. I'm anxiously awaiting your visit. Also Evelyn is coming to see me while I'm at basic. Yes siree, I'm really in love with that gal, OK now Pop, quit that laughing, I'm serious! It sure looks like I am going to enjoy basics.

It rained all night last night so I stayed here and played the radio. Heard the Hit Parade for the first time in weeks, ol' Frank Sinatra really has the women at his feet, I heard the reason all the gals swooned when he sang was because he sang with his fly open!!! Could be—could be!

One of my buddies who worked in the office saw my flying grades turned in by my instructor. He said the marks were good, and the instructor had said I was above average and a lot of things like that. Well, gotta go eat now and then we have to turn in our equipment.

The Bee's a busy little soul
and has no time for birth control
and that is why in times like these
you see so many sons of B's

With this little ditty, I'll close this letter. I'll write my address as soon as I get to Gunter. All my love,
Cobby

REFERENCES

[1] "Into the Sky: Primary Flying School." The Official Website of the National Museum of the USAF. Accessed May 29, 2011. http://www.nationalmuseum.af.mil/factsheets/factsheet. asp?id=1649.

2   Stearman PT-13D Kaydet and Photo. The Official Website of the National Museum of the USAF. Accessed May 29, 2011. http://www.nationalmuseum.af.mil/factsheets/ factsheet.asp?id=499.

3   Republic P-47D and Photo. The Official Website of the National Museum of the USAF. Accessed May 30, 2011. http://www.nationalmuseum.af.mil/factsheets/factsheet.asp?id=520

CHAPTER SEVEN

Crossroads, January 1944

Cobby was shipped to Gunter Field in Montgomery, Alabama, and was well on his way to fulfilling his dream of becoming a pilot, although the fear of washing out was always on his mind. At Maxwell he learned the fundamentals of flying an airplane, but now he would receive seventy hours of flight training in an airplane of greater weight, horsepower, and speed and would learn how to fly at night, by instruments, in formation and cross-country from one point to another. Also, for the first time, Cobby would operate a plane equipped with a two-way radio and a two-pitch propeller. At this point it would be decided whether Cobby would go to single-engine or twin-engine advanced flying school.

Although correspondence between Evelyn and Cobby had obviously been steady since they met in Nashville six months ago, she did not save his letters until he reached Gunter Air Field. Cobby made his intentions of marrying Evelyn well known since he met her in Nashville. This young couple dated for six weeks while Cobby was stationed in Nashville, and they got to know each other through written correspondence, not telephone calls, or emails, or Skype, or even visits together. They shared bits of themselves with open hearts on blank sheets of paper on an almost daily basis. During this time of great uncertainty, life was about loving and living in the moment, every hour and every day, and taking risks to find joy without the fear of rejection.

The following two photographs were taken from *Gunter Field—Alabama*, a booklet about cadet life published for the Army Air Forces in 1943 by E.M. Berry, Montgomery, Alabama.

The Wings of Gunter

January 22, 1944

Dearest Family,

I got here last week and I've been on the go ever since. I'm in a twin engine squadron, just the thing I didn't want, but that means that maybe I'll go to a twin engine advanced and be a buzz boy in a pea-shooter. Maybe things will work out to the best advantage if I can fly this B.T.! I only have 2 hrs to my credit, and when you're flying you *have a sense of power. The controls are very sensitive and ½ inch of stick in either direction* will lay it over on its side. You can hardly detect movement of the controls and instruments—whew! More stuff to remember, trim tabs flaps, mixture control, prop pitch and flight instruments galore. I sure have a time remembering what to do.

The barracks are pretty nice, but terribly crowded, 7 guys in our room, but all the guys in my room are OK. The food is super, the best I've had since I've been in the Air Corps.

Ninety percent of the guys in my group are French and can't speak English, but the squadron I'm in is all American.

Well, gotta study a little on this procedure of the B.T. so I'll write again soon as I get time. All my love, Cobby

"The BT-13 sure is a lotta plane with a powerful engine that is fast and more darn stuff to learn. Boy, I sure hope I don't have trouble with this baby."
[Cobby Webb]

The "Valiant" is a basic trainer representing the second of the three stages of pilot training—primary, basic and advanced. This airplane is considerably more complex than the PT-17 with a more powerful engine that is faster and heavier. In addition, the student pilot is required to use two-way communications with the ground, operate landing flaps, and a variable pitch propeller.

January 31, 1944

Dearest Family,
    Well, I'm anxiously awaiting your visit down here next week! I have a room for you all in the Whitley Hotel. Now everything will be OK if the weather holds up and I don't have to fly next Sunday.
    I'm having a pretty tough time learning how to fly this B.T. I haven't soloed yet and I have a little over eight hours. I just can't land the thing. I think I have the situation straightened out now and I expect to solo tomorrow. Boy! I really like to fly this ol' B.T. It really is a good plane, but so much stuff to do when you land and take off, you could use about three extra hands and feet.

Evelyn called me last night and she's coming down the week after you all. Now if I can only learn to fly this plane, and with you all and Evie coming down, I oughta have a right nice stay here. Hey, I got the ring Monday, and believe you me I'm really crazy about it. I show it off all the time.

Write soon. All my love, Cobby

February 10, 1944

Dearest Family,

I sure was glad that you all got to come down when you did. I sure was glad to see you. I trust you had a pleasant trip back home. I hope you enjoyed visiting with me as much as I enjoyed having you.

This week I've started flying instruments and have almost 5 hours on them—talk about something rough that requires intense concentration. They put you under a hood and you take off and fly around under there. Of course you don't have much time thinking about how hard it is because you're too busy watching the maze of instruments in front of you. You can't waste more than a second on any one instrument or all the rest will start going crazy. You sit there—your eyes moving constantly from instrument to instrument, her speed 120, artificial horizon centered, needle and ball zero, rate of climb zero, as you watch each instrument you keep saying over, and over to yourself, take it easy, take it easy, relax!!! Watch it now, use pressure on the controls instead of movement. Whew! What an ordeal, you climb out of the plane bathed in sweat, thanking God you didn't do any worse than you did, and all in all feeling pretty good, because you thought you didn't do too bad. Then your instructor climbs out, looks at you sadly and then starts telling you how terrible you are. You stand there with a stricken look on your face,

**till he walks off indignantly. Then you grin, shrug your
shoulders—all in a day's work. Cobby**

All the letters up until this point were written by Cobby to his parents
back home in West Virginia. These letters mention flying and share Cobby's
experiences, feelings, disappointments, setbacks, and fears. They also vividly
describe Cobby's love for Evelyn.

Now, saved love letters to Evelyn—*"My Darling Evelyn"*—enter the mix,
along with letters to the family in St. Albans, and reveal Cobby's intense
desire to be with her and his dejection when his plans are changed due to
his flight schedule.

February 11, 1944

My Darling Evelyn,
   *I sure was glad to hear you on the phone last night.
Golly, I sure wish I didn't have to fly Sunday. I found
out today we're going to fly all day Saturday, Sunday,
Monday, and Tuesday. I'll be a wreck in nothing flat!
Golly, I sure am disappointed that I have to fly this
week-end and don't get to see you. I've been planning
on this week-end a long time and have never had such
lousy luck in my life. Golly, Ev, I wanta see you so darn
bad it hurts. I can't even begin to tell you how much I
love you in these letters. So darlin' keep hopin' that we'll
get a chance to see each other before I leave here. I sure
hope so, 'cause I have a lotta stuff to talk over with you.*
   *Hey Evelyn, what d'you mean by tellin' that gal we
were married? Don't you know that's how nasty rumors
get started? You'd better tell her different or you might
be embarrassed one of these days! Evelyn, have you told
your folks about how we feel toward each other? Gotta
go now, hon, I love you forever, Cobby*

February 24, 1944

Dearest Family,

Please forgive me for not writing but I have been busy flying. Incidentally, I have almost 60 hours now and I only need ten more, plus a check ride and instrument check. My instructor told us today he thought we could pass the instrument check. He has more faith in me than I do. He might be satisfied with my instrument flying, but I'll be durned if I am. Learning to fly those instruments may mean the difference of life and death for me some day, and you can bet your life that I want to live.

I started formation flying yesterday and boy, is that fun. We fly a "V" type formation in an element of three. That takes just about as much concentration as flying instruments but not quite. Boy, do those other planes look close. We're about 5 feet away from each other and brother that's close, when you're flying at 130 m.p.h. Well, if nothing happens I'll be leaving here in a few weeks for Advanced. I sure hope I can do OK and get there. I think there's been about 6 guys wash outa our class, and there's bound to be a few more, but I doubt if more than 10 or 15 more guys will wash out.

Hey Clayton, what gives on this athletic situation? I guess you're a pretty hot ball player, but for gosh sakes don't let it go to your head. When you're playing competitive sports, forget everything else except the game you're playing. Play with everything you've got, and above all, keep in good physical condition. If you do these things Clate ol' boy, I'll be reading about you in the All-American line up in a few years. All my love, Cobby

February 28, 1944

My darling Evelyn,

    Honey, first of all I want to tell you how much I love you. I hope you don't mind, I only wish I was there so I could tell you instead of writing it.

    We only have about 10 more days to go before we graduate. I only have to get about 10 more hours of night flying and then I'll be there. I don't know when we'll get furlough, but I hope it's soon after we graduate.

    I went over to the tailor shop today and tried on my uniforms. Just tween you n' me I look pretty sharp. Pardon the conceit. We've been buying up parts of our uniforms like mad the last couple of days. I picked up a sharp, Bancroft Flighter hat yesterday, and when I'm in my room, I put it on and get a little mirror time.

    Just think, darling, after fifteen months I've almost finished. Golly, I think I'd go crazy if I washed out now. I start night flying tonight, and if I can stay on the beam and not have any accidents I'll be "in." Now, if I'm made a Flight Officer, I'll be just about the happiest guy in the world. Wings and bars, a furlough slip in my pocket and on my way to see the most wonderful gal in the world. That's the day I'm anxiously awaiting. Last night my ol' buddy Dave and I sat up till midnight telling each other what swell gals we were in love with. Boy, was I blue when I finally went to bed. I went to sleep thinking about you, dreamt about you, and when I woke up you were the first thing I thought of. I must admit, my darling, you are uppermost in my mind 24 hours a day!

    This class is supposed to get pretty good assignments after graduation. They say about 90% of the class is going to get either P-51's or P-47's for combat. Everyone is pretty excited about our future, me included. Gotta go now sweetheart. Remember—I love you, Cobby

February 29, 1944

My Darling Evelyn,
 Golly, I don't know what to say at all. I feel pretty bad about the call I made to you tonight. Honestly, if I'd have known you were going to get sore at me the way you did, I would have never called you. Now look, before you fly off and do something we'll both be sorry for, let me explain. When I called, I didn't think I'd even get the call thru, 'cause I didn't have much time. I had to be out on the flight line at six o'clock to begin night flying, but it so happened that the call went right thru and I got to talk to you. I didn't have enough change for a person to person call, so I called station to station. And I hung up like I did because my three minutes were up and I didn't have anymore dough. And about that ring, you didn't expect me to cart that thing all over the country, did you? And take a chance on losing it or having it stolen. Well, if you did, I'm sorry I disappointed you. And another thing—do you think I'm trying to keep you from coming down here? It's not my fault that I have to fly on week-ends. As far as I am concerned, they can shove this flying up their you know what! (I'll explain in detail after we're married.) I want to see you as bad as you wish to see me, I wouldn't be surprised if I didn't want to see you more, but that's beside the point, what I'm gettin' at is that I'm just another flunky in Uncle Sam's army and he dictates the terms of my existence, not me! I'm doing my damndest to get a week-end for us, but as long as I have to fly, I'm going to fly, and that's that! Now that's settled, I love you, baby, and don't you ever forget it. Well, honey, I gotta hit the hay now, I'll be dreaming about you in a few minutes. I can hardly wait. I love you, Cobby

March 2, 1943

My Darling Evelyn,

   Honey, I just wanta tell you right now before I say another word, that I love you more than anything. I want to tell you how happy I am that you're writing so often. I come in from flying and I'm all pooped out, then I read a letter from you and I'm not so tired anymore. And remember even if I don't write so much, my every thought is of you. Don't fear that I don't love you, because, Evelyn, I do, more than I ever thought was possible for anyone to love another. I'll try my darndest to write more often.

   Hey Baby, yes, I think about what I'm going to do after the war. If I make the grade and get my wings and outlive the war, I'm going to try and get a connection with an airline. But there's liable to be thousands of guys in the Air Corps like me with the same idea in mind. If so, I don't know what I'll do. I'd sure like to retire after the war and just love you!

   Boy, am I tired tonite, I believe I'm getting pilots fatigue, and I'm almost sick of flying. We flew all day today and I got 5 hours in, and believe you me I can hardly sit down. It's just about as bad as if I'd been in the saddle all day. I dread every ride. Only time I have any fun is when I go up by myself. But I'll be OK as soon as I get a little rest. In the meantime, I love you, Cobby

March 4, 1944

My darling Evelyn,

   Sorry I've delayed writing you this week, but it's the same old story. I havta fly. We're up to schedule and it's rumored that we'll get next week-end off if we keep up. I started formation flying yesterday and is it fun. You're about 5 feet away from the [other] plane, doing turns, climbs, dives and everything all in formation. There are three plane elements in a "v" type formation. You gotta watch what you're doing 'cause a slip can mean a nasty crack-up. Yep, honey, I'm doing OK in my flying. I think. At least my instructor doesn't fuss at me as much as he used to. I hope I can pass the rest of my checks. I have a 40-hr and instrument coming up.

Honey, I wish you wouldn't write letters to me in bed, and tell me that you wish I were there, 'cause it gets me all sexed up and frustrated, if you know what I mean. Boy, if you were here now I believe I'd just eat you up. I'd like to love you till I fell over. Do you know what, I love you baby, and that's no jive. I think about you 23 hrs and 59 ½ minutes a day and can hardly wait for your visit next week.

Please excuse the briefness of this letter but I got lots of stuff to do before hitting the hay. But no matter how short my letters, "I'll always love you." Cobby

March 13, 1944

Dearest Family,

I guess you think I'm pretty much of a no-good for not writing, but I have the same excuse—busy flying. I have 75 hours and I only need about three or four more and I'll be finished, but I have a couple of checks to take yet, and I'm still not outa the woods as far as basic is concerned.

But enough of this, I have something to tell you that I hope will make you as happy as me. You're going to have a daughter in law. Yep, your ol' Cobweb's engaged. Evelyn came down this weekend, and before she could say no, I had the ring on her, but she didn't wanta say no. We're undecided as to when the wedding is going to be. Not until after I get my wings at any rate, maybe after the war's over, don't know yet. Maybe you all can give us some advice. One thing I want you all to remember is "you haven't lost a son, but you've gained a daughter," and I know you'll be as crazy about her as I am. We had a wonderful weekend, and Pop, if you're wondering, we didn't do anything wrong, if you get what I mean.

Well, I gotta go now. Guess what we're going to do? You know to keep us, "nervous in the service," we're going to drill, XXX###000!!! All my love, Cobby

P.S. Sending $20 to finish payment on ring. Is that enough?

March 15, 1944

Hello Darling,

I don't know how I can tell you how much I love you, after having you in my arms just two short days ago. But I'll try. I sure hope you enjoyed your visit with me as much as I enjoyed having you. Golly baby, I feel like a new man, no kiddin'. I'm so happy. I go around telling all the guys I know, that I'm engaged! Engaged to the sweetest girl in the whole world. Everyone I tell gives me the ol' glad hand, y'know, the happy five. Boy, I feel fine!

I wrote my folks and told them about us. I know they'll be as happy as I am. By the way, honey, what did your mother say about your impending marriage? I hope she doesn't mind too much.

By and by, honey, we're gonna get hitched. I'm still undecided as to when we'll tie the knot. The more I think about it, the more I think we should give the idea of marriage a very careful consideration. I know right now I don't have a cent in the bank. Maybe we should have a little more security in the form of greenbacks. What do you think? Also maybe our parents should have a hand in deciding when we take the final step.

Well, darlin' I guess I'd better shove off, gotta hit the hay now. I flew 4 ½ hours this afternoon.

Believe me baby, I can hardly sit down, and that's an understatement. Write soon, I love you. Cobby

March 18, 1944

Hello Darling,

Couldn't write last night after you called because I had to go to a War Orientation lecture and discussion. We had an open discussion on all topics pertaining to war, supervised by our tactical officer.

Sure glad you called to let me know you thought we should wait a while before we get married. I think the main reason we should wait is my present financial situation, which is, by the way, nil! Another thing is our age, pretty young to rush right into marriage with nothing but our love to live on, but living on love isn't such a bad idea, though, the only thing wrong is that it isn't practical.

Honey, don't worry about what I asked you about having an affair. I just asked 'cause there aren't many gals today who can say that they haven't. Besides, it wouldn't affect my love for you if you had, but I'm sure glad you didn't.

Baby doll, I've been thinking about us all day, as soon as I get my wings and a furlough (both I hope), we'll take off and go home to good ol' West Virginia. When and if I do get to go home, it'll really be wonderful 'cause it'll be around the end of May or the first of June, and it's really beautiful back home that time of the year and I've been thinking of a hundred and one things we can do to enjoy ourselves. Well, Evelyn, my sweet, I have to hit the hay now. I'll love you forever, Cobby

P.S. Give my very best regards to my future mother and father-in-law.

March 20, 1944

My Darling Evelyn,
How's my baby getting along? I hope you're OK and honey I think we're doing the best thing by waiting a while before we get married. Ordinarily, I don't approve of long engagements, but in our case I can discover no other solution. As soon as I get my wings (I hope) and save a little money, we'll get married.

Well, yesterday I finished my flying in basic training. No more flying until I get to Advanced. We leave this coming Friday, I think. I don't know where I'm going, and I don't even know whether I'm going to single or twin engine advanced training schools. I sure hope it's single!

I gotta letter from home yesterday and Dad congratulated me very heartily, and said if I was sure I love you (which I am) that getting engaged met with his wholehearted approval. He wasn't surprised tho 'cause he knew I was going to offer you a ring as soon as you came down. He knew because he brought it down to me when he came to see me here. I gotta go now, so be real sweet and remember, darling. I love you, Cobby

March 21, 1944

Dearest Family,
First of all, I guess you'll want to know about my training. I know you'll be happy to know that I've

finished my basic training here and that I'm now waiting to be shipped to Advanced which will probably be either Turner or Craig Field, both of which are in Alabama, around 150 miles from here. I asked for single engine, because I have that yearning that as a kid I haven't outgrown, and that's speed! And more speed! Don't think I'll be sent to single engine tho because of my height and weight, limits are 6 ft tall and 175 lbs, while I'm 6' ¾" and 180 lbs. Keep your fingers crossed for me because I might get thru on a waiver.

Glad you all feel as you do about my engagement. I guess you were sort of surprised when Evelyn wrote & told you about making plans to be married as soon as I got my wings. To be frank I was more than surprised. I was downright scared that she was going ahead and making plans that I couldn't get out of, so I wrote and told her we should wait. She wrote and told you we're going to wait, didn't she? Well, if you didn't know, you know now.

Hey, I saw in the paper that Stu Holcomb is going to be drafted, and him with two kids, too. Well, it sure looks like things are drawing to a head, and believe me I'm sure thankful I've been on this side of the pond for so long. I've come to the conclusion that the marines are doing the fighting in this war, and take it from me, I don't envy them a bit.

Here's something that might interest you concerning the "British fighting to the last." Of all the flyers in the R.A.F. before the Battle of Britain, only six of the whole original outfit lived from start to finish. That's what Churchill meant when he said "never has so much been owed to so few." All my love, Cobby

P.S. FLASH! I just saw my shipping orders. Going to single engine 26th at Craig Field, Selma Alabama

The pilots who survived the two-month Battle of Britain were known as "The Few." However, Cobby's claim that only six pilots survived

was not accurate. The Battle of Britain was fought in the air in the late summer of 1940 between the Royal Air Force and Luftwaffe fighters, who outnumbered the RAF three to one and had veteran and experienced pilots. By this time in World War II, Germany's army had swept through Europe and occupied many countries, including Austria, Poland, Denmark, Belgium, and had recently forced France to surrender. The Germans had their eyes on England next, but in order for the German Luftwaffe to invade England, they had to first destroy the Royal Air Force Fighter Command guarding the coast of Great Britain. The Luftwaffe was a powerful air force and the Royal Air Force Fighter Command had a smaller fighter group made up of young and inexperienced fighter pilots. Toward the end of this conflict, pilots from Belgium, Poland, and Czechoslovakia who fled their countries after German domination joined in the fight. This battle lasted four months and would become the only battle fought entirely in the air. Some days there were four to five aircraft missions. Over 540 RAF pilots would lose their lives, but they stopped Germany from dominating all of Northern Europe. At the end of the battle, Winston Churchill said: "Never in the field of human conflict was so much owed by so many to so few."

March 21, 1944

Hello Darling,

How's my Baby tonite? Well, I'm off to Advanced at Craig Field in Selma, Alabama, and honey, guess what? It's single engine. Boy, that's really terrific, that's what I wanted and for once luck was with me. Oh joy!

Haven't flown much in the last three or four days as I'm finished. Tomorrow I have to fly across country as an observer. It's a student team ride and the guy I fly with flies under the hood on instruments. All I have to do is sit up front and watch that he doesn't run into anything. Didn't do a thing today. Man, it was wonderful. I hate to say it but I believe your fiancé (me) is just a trifle lazy. No cracks! But can I help it if I'm tired all of the time? Anyhow, I enjoy lying on my back all day.

How's your Mother and Dad, Baby? Give them both my regards and thank them for me for taking care of my dearest one.

Oh yes, Baby, before I say anything else, I wanta wish you a Happy Birthday and many more returns. Did you have a good time at your party tonite? Write me soon darling. In the meantime I love you, Cobby

March 23, 1944

Hello Darling,

Well, in two more days 'ol Cobweb will be on his way to Craig Field in Selma Ala. Boy! I sure am glad that I got to go to single engine Advanced. I might get to be a buzz boy yet. Believe it or not, I have a secret ambition to fly a P-51 Mustang. Man alive, give me one of those and a couple of good wing men, and lookout Luftwaffe. A guy with one of these babies is really terrific, and there's no stopping him.

Tonite we're having a graduation dance, to celebrate our graduation from basic training. Here it is 9:30 already and I haven't even gone yet. Of course, I'm only going to get something to eat. Also if you're burning with curiosity (I can see you now) just to relieve your agony, I'm going by myself. Stag—alone, get it. Remember, above everything else, I love you. Cobby

REFERENCES

1   Vultee BT-13 Valiant. The Official Website of the National Museum of the USAF. Accessed May 30, 2011. http://www.nationalmuseum.af.mil/factsheets/factsheet.asp?id=481.

2 "Always Remembered . . . Never Forgotten." The Official Website of the Battle of Britain Historical Society. Accessed April 30, 2012. http://battleofbritain1940.net/bobhsoc.

CHAPTER EIGHT

Winning His Wings

Cobby was very happy to be going to Craig Field in Alabama for Advanced Flying School, since this part of the training prepared cadets for the kind of plane they would fly in combat. Cobby had always wanted to fly a single engine fighter plane and was looking forward to the next nine weeks. He would be flying in an AT-6 airplane, learn aerial gunnery and combat maneuvers, and increase his skills in navigation and instrument flying. After completing this training, Cobby would finally receive his wings and commission to be the "hot pilot" he always wanted to be.

March 27, 1944

Hello Darling,
Well, been here since Friday, and so far things haven't been too bad. But starting tomorrow things are going to pick up. We go to the Flight Line tomorrow morning for the first time. Boy, I'm sure looking forward to flying this AT-6 plane. From what I've heard, this is really a sweet plane. I met a couple of guys here who just got their wings and are now flying P-40's here, and from what they say, there's nothing to flying this plane. Boy, I sure hope I can get those bars and wings.
Darling, guess what? I love you more and more every day. I've been thinking about you quite a bit since you were down, and the more I think about it, the more I hope I get to be an instructor. Then we could get married. Boy! I sure would like that. Just think me n' you, living together out in town some place, and me getting up in the morning and coming back at nite, just like a civilian job. Now tell me, Sweetheart, would you or would you not like that set up?
Sorry I haven't written sooner, but we've been pretty darn busy getting settled and getting our equipment.

Tomorrow night we have a big stand-by inspection. What a pain in the back that is going to be. But the sooner things get started around here, the sooner they are going to end, and that's the day I'm looking forward to.

Take care of yourself, Evelyn, my sweet, and don't worry about me. Whenever you get to feelin' blue and lousy, remember I feel the same way and I love you with all my heart, Cobby

AT-6 Texan

Courtesy of National Museum of the U.S. Air Force
"This is really a sweet plane." [Cobby Webb]

The AT-6 is the single engine advanced trainer for all Allied student pilots that flew in World War II. Although it was not as fast as a fighter, this plane had good maneuverability and was easy to handle and repair. A pilot's airplane, it could roll, loop, spin, snap, and vertical roll and was designed to give the best possible training in all types of tactics, from ground strafing to bombardment and aerial dogfighting. This plane had it all—blind-flying instrumentation, gun and standard cameras, fixed and flexible guns, and just about every other device that military pilots had to operate. No wonder Cobby looked forward to flying this machine.

April 1, 1944

Hello Darling,

Well, here I am at Craig Field all set to go. We start flying Tuesday and until then we're using all the time getting settled.

Today we had our G-4 physical examination—that's the stiffest physical test the army gives anyone. It consists of eye, ear, throat, nose, blood test, the same physical we had at the Classification Center. We came down here on buses and trucks. Just my luck that I got a truck and spent a very uncomfortable hour and a half on my "posturus extremus."

Honey, I'm sure sorry you sprained your ankle, but you know how trompin' and stompin' with those G.I. dogfaces, anything is liable to happen to you. Speaking of dancing, baby, I'm listening to the Hit Parade and now they're playing "Don't Sweetheart Me." Sure wish you were here, we'd really do some rug cutting and I don't mean perhaps!

We're being quarantined for two weeks while we're here, and after that I guess we'll be too busy flying to think about open post. Oh yes, baby, you know where most of these guys go from here after graduation? Last class all but 40 men out of 200 were made instructors in basic and advanced schools. The forty cadets who weren't made instructors took training in P-40's; here for two weeks and then on to other transition schools. I hope I'm one of the chosen few to take P-40 training, but I don't care if I am made an instructor, 'cause that gives us a chance to get married!!!

Frank Sinatra is singing "I Love You" now and believe me, darling, that expresses my sentiments to you exactly. I sure hope you can come down here, I'm keeping my fingers crossed, and I'm hoping things will work out like they did while I was at Gunter. Well, sweetheart, I guess I'll get ready for bed. Sure wish you were here and darling, I'll love you forever, Cobby

April 5, 1944

Dearest Family,

I just have time to write a quick letter. We're really on a rugged schedule and I hardly have time to sit down for a minute.

I'm having a pretty tough time learning how to fly this aeroplane. The procedures just about drive me crazy. I only have 5 hrs. to my credit, but I hope to solo in the next couple of rides. I don't have much confidence in either myself or the airplane. It's really a tough job to land. It has a very strong ground looping characteristic due to the closeness of the landing gear. Just between you n' me I don't trust these retractable landing gear too much, but they have very few accidents in these planes. I saw a P-40 slide in on its belly the other day. He couldn't get his wheels down so he slid in, made a very good landing, too, and with minimum damage to the plane. Didn't hurt him a bit.

There are a lot of rumors floating around here as to the wash out rate. I know that it's going to be plenty high in our class. You get washed out for the slightest thing. Boy, I'm hopin' and prayin' that I'll get a few good breaks, so I can get through OK. It would make me bitter as the devil if I washed out after having gone this far. I'll do the best I can and if that isn't good enough, I don't guess I belong in the air.

Got measured up for a uniform the other day, and the bare essentials cost almost $250 and the Govt. only gives us $250 clothing allotment. Well, folks, gotta go now, the bugle blows at 5:30 and it takes all of my roommates to get me outa bed. Write often. All my love, Cobby

April 6, 1944

Hello Darling,

 Sorry I haven't written sooner but things haven't been going so good for ol' Cobweb. I'm worried to death that I'm going to wash out. You know they don't need so many pilots now as they did a few months ago, so now they are washing guys out for the slightest mistake. If you have an accident, even of the most insignificant kind, you're washed. So darling keep your fingers crossed for ol' Cobweb. I have about 5 hours dual now, and I'll be soloing pretty soon if nothing happens.

 You know what, baby, I love you. Yep, it's the truth, and I just can't help it. I want those wings so bad, not only for myself but for you. If I get those wings, we can be married a helluva lot sooner than if I don't. So Evelyn, cross your fingers and keep hoping I can get there. If I wash out now, I doubt if I'll ever be the same.

 I haven't been doing much except work. They're really tough on us down here. I got 9 tours last week just for the condition of the room. So I won't be doing much for the next couple of weeks, except walking 'em off. But darling, don't you worry because a couple of my roommates have over 15 tours a piece. In fact between the four of us in my room we have 50 tours between us.

 Evelyn, I don't think you're going to get to come down here because I'm so busy, and when we graduate, the ceremony only lasts 5 minutes and they have it at 5:30 in the morning. They don't even give you the wings then. We were measured for uniforms Sunday. Sure hope I get to wear it as a pilot. I'll love you forever.
Cobby

April 7, 1944

Hello Darling,
   I just have a few minutes to dash off this letter, so please forgive me if it is short. I got your cute Easter card tonight which reminds me I got you some perfume, the only thing I could get on the post. And I'm sorta afraid to send it to you 'cause it's just a trifle loud if you know what I mean. But I'll take a chance to send it to you as soon as I can get it ready.
   Well, I have about 7 hours to my credit now, and I haven't soloed yet, but I have hopes to do so in the next couple of days, probably my next flight.
   We had a big dance last night out at the Selma Country Club. We were allowed to stay out there until ten thirty. I got to hit the ol' sack about 11:30, then I crawled out at 5:30 this morning. So you can imagine how I felt this morning when I went into the air at just about dawn, but getting back to the dance. It's about a 15-minute ride from the post here across town, and we went over in G.I. trucks. The whole class of 44E was supposed to go but only about 150 went. Well, when we got there everyone piled outa the trucks and rushed into the club, and there were all these beautiful gals lined up around the wall. No one gave the girls a second glance but rushed right into the bar. Of course, I was right up there fighting like mad to order something refreshing, and I don't mean Cokes. They had a pretty good band so I sat around listening to it and thinking of you. Boy, when I start thinking about you I get blue as hell. That's gotta go, I guess you realize that don'tcha, and that means—marriage, in the near future, too! So for a while, sweetheart, I'll close with—Loving you forever,
Cobby

April 10, 1944

Dearest Family,

Here it is Easter Sunday and we just got back from the flight line, although we had the morning off and could sleep until eleven. I've been sorta blue, I would have given anything to get home and be with you all. Did you get the corsage I sent, Mom? I didn't send it personally but had a friend who was fortunate to get out last night do it for me.

Now about coming down for my graduation, if I graduate! I know they have very little pomp and ceremony, and what little they do have (5 minutes) takes place at 0530 and that's early, civilian, army or otherwise. So don't make any extensive plans until I let you know of the surety of my graduation. Don't be surprised if I wash out, 'cause they washed almost a third of 44D class ahead of me, and they're really getting rough. They expect the very best, and little things count a lot in their book. You know the Army doesn't need and doesn't want pilots now, so they're washing them out everywhere, even in pre-flight. Don't worry, though, if I do wash out it will be because I'm liable to kill myself if they let me through!

Well, I gotta go now, I hope this answers your questions, Pop, and I do read your letters and I do enjoy them and I do expect them and I do look forward to them, and I don't want you to cease them. All my love, Cobby

April 21, 1944

My Darling Evelyn,

I guess I'm in the dog house again for not writing more often. Don't be too hard on me, sweetheart, 'cause I've really been busy. We haven't flown all week but we sure have been getting our fill of lectures, on everything.

The weather here has been terrible—rain and fog with a very low ceiling, so low that even the birds are walking.

The upper class graduated Saturday and they had a pretty nice ceremony. I hope that they have one for us! Only about 40 guys were made instructors and the rest of the class are going to be fighter pilots. I doubt if very many of our fellows get to be instructors. I guess you know they've closed up a bunch of primary schools.

I've been taking tests all week to decide whether I'll be a flight officer or a 2nd Lt. I hope I did OK. I don't mind being a F.O. but I'd rather be a 2nd Lt.

You know what, Evelyn? I love ya, yep I just can't help it. The more I think about you the more I love you. No kidding, when I start thinking about you, I almost go into a trance. I know I'm in a daze half the time. The only time I don't think about you is when I'm flying. And the only reason I don't think of you there is because if I did, I might forget where I was, and I might step out for a pack of cigarettes at 10,000 feet and that would be bad!

I gotta go now, so baby, be careful and remember above everything else in the world, I love you. Cobby

April 24, 1944

Dearest Family,

I hope all of you are well and happy. I'm fine and so far I'm doing OK in my flying. I only have about 20 hours to my credit because of the terrible weather we're having. It's rained every day this week and I mean rain! I'm doing formation work, when I do get up, lotta fun, but you have to concentrate so much it really tires you out. After a couple of hours formation, I'm just about ready to hit the ol' sack.

We had a bunch of exams last week to determine whether or not we'll be flight officers or Second Looie's. Myself, I'm betting on the F.O. We had a

lecture from our group C.O. yesterday and the way
he talked, you gotta be pretty hot to get thru here. He
said, "We're training you men to be killers, and if you
can't be a good killer, you aren't worth a damn, and
I'll make sure you wash out." I never did think much
about the killin' part of the Air Corps, but he's right.
I wonder what's going to become of these so called
"killers" after the war, when they're turned loose with
nothing to kill? There's a thought that takes a lot of
thinking!

I'd better close now, gotta get up to fly at 05:00 in
the morn. Oh, how I hate to get up in the morning. All
my love, Cobby

May 1, 1944

My Darling Evelyn,

*I've just finished reading your letter so I decided
that I'd better write immediately! Darling, you gave
me an awful scare when you told me about that close
call you had Saturday night. For gosh sakes, honey, be
careful. An automobile accident is a heck of a lot more
dangerous than a crack up in one of these AT-6's. Now,
I'll have something else to worry about! Oh, before
I forget it, what do you mean that you're glad we're
waiting "indefinitely" before we get married? Not sorry
you're engaged, are ya? God, I hope not. I wish you
wouldn't use that word indefinitely. You make it sound
like never.*

*Things around here are in a pretty sad state—work,
work, my God, I'm getting punchy. Besides that, when
we do get open post, I have about fifty million tours to
walk off. It seems like every time I try to get eager, the
more I get in trouble. If I can only last about a month
more I'll be OK. We are supposed to graduate the 23rd
of May, but if the weather doesn't clear up soon, we'll
have to finish our training AFTER we get our wings and*

commission, and that will delay our furloughs (if we get any) quite a while.

Today we had a cross country up to way past Birmingham. I came in with about 10 gallons of gas. I had about fifteen more minutes of flying time left. Don't think I wasn't relieved when I finally saw the field, but don't get me wrong. I wasn't lost, just a little off course was all.

We started instrument flying last week and if it is anything I hate, it's instrument flying. It's pretty rough, too. I've been having a helluva time! They washed out one of the guys in my section today. And from what I understand they're going to get about 8 or 10 more before we get thru. Sweetheart, keep your fingers crossed for the kid!

What did they do to the Nashville Classification Center? Make it into a Rehabilitation Center? Don't work too hard, baby. You know I might be in one of those camps one of these days.

Honey, guess what? Yep, you're right, I love ya and I can't keep my mind off you and sometimes it's rather embarrassing, 'cause everytime I get a pen or pencil in my hand I keep writing "Evelyn" or "Miss Groves" and sometimes I have quite a time explaining. Baby, I sure wish I was there to give you some of those special kisses you were talking about and to receive some of your wonderful lovin'. Of course you realize that you're the only gal in this world that I love more than anything, and the longer I'm away, the more I love you.

I guess I'd better sign out now. You know, the ol' sack is callin' me. I gotta get up in the morning to go out to the flight line. This life is really telling on me. I got circles down to my chin. Write soon, darling, and remember, Evelyn, I love you. Cobby

May 10, 1944

Dearest Family,

I guess you all are just about ready to disown me for not writing, but these past two weeks have really been rugged. We've been flying four and five hours, not once in a while, but every day. Already five guys have washed out in our squadron, and probably a couple more before our class graduates.

I have the maximum number of hours in instrument flying and I haven't passed my instrument or 50-3 check yet. I don't know what'll happen. We've had 5 cross country in the last few days, most of them around three hundred miles round trip. You gotta be really on the ball 'cause you can't get very lost when you don't have much gas left. There are a lot of radio beams around here, and you can get a radio fix using these beams, and can determine your position within a mile. We only have two more weeks to go and if I can just keep from cracking up a ship, I think I can make it.

We had a pretty bad crack up yesterday which could have been avoided if the guys in the plane had kept their heads. As it was, they went into a spin at 1,000 ft and couldn't recover because of confusion. Consequently, both were killed, an instructor and a student of the lower class, a kid I knew just to speak to.

I'm pretty lucky to come to a single engine advanced school, 'cause when 44F took their physical they segregated all of the men who were over 5 ft and 10 in. and sent them to a twin engine school, in Illinois. They sent thirty-five men up there and sent thirty-five midgets here. Boy, they look like half-men.

Well, we start night flying in a couple of days and we have to fly cross-country at night, too. One thing about flying at night, it's a lot easier to land because you don't have all that heat coming off the runways. On these hot days, the heat coming off the runways keeps you from hitting the runway when you should. About the only thing to do is make a wheel landing. Well, I gotta go. It has taken me 2 days to write this. All my love, Cobby

May 10, 1944

My Darling Evelyn,
    Well, by now I guess you're just about ready to cut my throat? But tell me, do you still love me, even though I haven't written for ages? Don't be too disgusted with me, I've been having a pretty rugged time for the past couple of weeks, and now that graduation day is nearly here, things are getting even rougher. Everyday we fly about four hours and when we're thru for the day I don't have energy enough to do anything but relax. I'm writing this in ground school and I can hardly keep my eyes open to do it.
    I have about 60 hrs to my credit now and all I have to do is night flying and finish up instruments and a little formation. I've flown twenty hours in the last five days. It may not sound like much but take it from me, that's the most work I've ever done in five days.
    Say baby, how are things getting along back Nashville way? I hope you're having a good time, but not too good. I've been on this post so dern long I think I'm getting attached to the place and don't guess I'll get out until I graduate (if and when).
    Oh yeah, before I forget, I want to tell you something. I've told you this I guess about a million times, but I hope you won't mind just this once, and this is what I have to say: I love you, darling, and even though I don't write very often, you can rest assured that my every thought is of you.
    Right now I'm in the middle of a movie. Of course it's a G.I. job on "Identification of Raiders." This one is on how to recognize disguised freighters etc., which in reality are surface raiders. Well, I'm in another class now, and we're getting another one of those darn movies. This time it's about P-47's so it won't be so bad.

As much as I hate to, darling, I guess I'll have to close, but sweetheart remember, I love you, Cobby
P.S. Only 13 more days to go. Keep your fingers crossed.

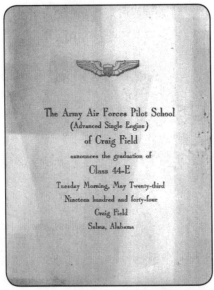

The Army Air Forces Pilot School
(Advanced Single Engine)
of Craig Field
announces the graduation of
Class 44-E
Tuesday Morning, May Twenty-third
Nineteen hundred and forty-four
Craig Field
Selma, Alabama

"Boy did it feel good to get my wings" [Cobby Webb]

Cobby Webb

"I'm one happy pilot" [Cobby Webb]

Cobby finally received his wings and commission for successfully completing pilot training. Completing pilot's training was a historically difficult and dangerous task in the Army Air Corps. Between January 1941 and August 1945, there were 191,654 cadets who were awarded their pilot wings and 132,993 air cadets who "washed out" or were killed during training, a loss rate of approximately 40 percent due to accidents, academic, or physical problems, and other causes.

With the graduation of Lieutenant Dana A. Webb from pilot school came a long-awaited furlough with Evelyn and a trip home to visit his family in West Virginia before returning for final preparations to go overseas.

June 7, 1944

Dearest Family,

Well, before starting off I'd like to try and tell you what a wonderful time I had while I was home. It was perfect and not a thing was lacking. I can't describe how much that short leave meant to me. I'll always have it among my treasured memories.

Evelyn and I got to Nashville about 3:30 Saturday afternoon after a very enjoyable trip. I didn't leave at two-thirty Sunday morning as planned, but caught the nine o'clock train Sunday morning and arrived at Craig at 10:00 that night, which made things OK.

I'm down at Eglin now. We came down on buses this morning, and what a desolate place this is—nothing but an auxiliary field set out in the middle of the sticks. The living quarters are pretty raw and the food is scarce and not very good so far. And they're still treating us like cadets!

You know what? I sure miss you all more than ever before and especially I miss Evelyn. Every day I realize how much more I love her as the days slip past. You know, I never knew I could love a girl as much as I love her. She's really terrific. I stayed all night with her and her folks Saturday night and they were really swell to me.

I'm rooming down here at Field # 6 with all my buddies from advanced, five of us in a little room. What a lot of fun we're having. We've just been discussing golf and I was telling the boys about us playing and the fun we had, Pop! All my love, Cobby

June 7, 1944

Hello Darling,
    I arrived well and not so happy in Selma last night about 10:00. I was pretty lucky 'cause I had a seat all the way from Nashville. Tomorrow we're leaving for Eglin Field, Fla. for gunnery and will be down there for about two or three weeks.
    I came in last night and all of my buddies had already gotten here and we had a big bull session before we went to sleep. You should hear some of the yarns these boys have to tell, man they'd slay you. Some of the guys got engaged, some married, and all of them stayed "tight" most of the time on leave.
    Darling, know what? I sure miss you, and I've never felt so lost in all my life. I can see you now standing up there in the station at Nashville. You looked so darn sweet. Evelyn, we gotta get married soon, and I ain't kiddin' a bit, I never realized that I love you so damned much until I spent that leave at home with you. Now I know I can't live without you. Honest, baby. I'm serious as hell. You may think this is pretty mushy, but if you only knew how I yearn for you now, you'd feel different. Tell me, darling, what are your views on the marriage situation? I hope you've come around to my way of thinking, that marriage for us should happen right away, as soon as possible, with no delay, etc. Well, Sweetheart, I gotta go and remember I love you. Cobby

June 13, 1944

My Darling Evelyn,

Got cha sweet ol' letter today, honey. Sure have been looking forward to it for a long time. It sure lifted my morale 100%.

Baby, don't think because of all that heavy courtin' we did, I think less of you, because if any thing it made me love you more, and I want you more than I ever did. I realize it was hard for you to stop, but I'm glad you did. I'm sure glad one of us has some sense. Baby, we have to get married, but quick! Darling—I love you, purely, simply, and with everything in me! And I won't ever stop loving you either, darling! One of these days, we'll be married, and live together the rest of our lives. Maybe this war will be over sooner than I think now that the invasion has started. Anyway, I hope so.

I must tell you that I'm getting 3 bucks a day more down here than I do otherwise, because I'm in detached service down here. And when I say detached, I mean it, this place is about 100,000,000 miles from no place.

Well, kid, things are getting tough down here now. We started aerial gunnery today and already some guy ran into the target tow cable and damn near tore a wing off. They washed him out and yesterday in ground gunnery, another guy hit the target and bent his prop on the target and scraped the ground doing 180 m.p.h. He didn't crack up but he also washed out. Keep your fingers crossed for ol' kid Cobweb.

I gotta go now, gotta get up at 05:00. Give my best to your mama and poppa and remember, darling, I love you. Cobby

June 15, 1943

Dearest Family,

I got your letters yesterday. I was beginning to think maybe you'd forgotten me. I'm down here at Eglin Field in Florida taking my gunnery training. We've already shot at stationery ground targets, now we're shooting at aerial targets which move at 120 m.p.h. Pretty rugged business and confidentially I stink when it comes to aerial gunnery. We get 200 shots and get to make fifteen passes. Well, my highest score has been fifteen hits out of 200. We have gun cameras mounted in harmonization with the guns, so we can look over our mistakes after a mission. My pictures look pretty good, but the results are terrible. I hope I get the knack soon so I can show myself that I can shoot. We only have a week left down here and am I glad. There isn't a thing to do but go to the movies every other night. It gets very boring just sitting around. I write a good many letters, but even that gets awfully tiresome. We only fly about an hour a day, but we're on the flight line about 6 hours just sitting around.

I'm sure glad that you all like Evelyn so much, and think that she'd make me a good wife and you a good swell daughter. Also glad that public opinion is high towards her. Yep, I sure do love that lil' ol' gal.

I guess I'll be starting P-40 training soon. Oh happy day.

Well, I gotta go get a big lecture because of the P.P. scores we've been shooting. Be seeing you. All my love,
Cobby

June 26, 1944

My Darling Evelyn,
    *This is ol' Cobweb in person. I'm now back at Craig
Field. I got thru gunnery OK, but just by the skin of my
teeth.*
    *We get checked out in P-40's tomorrow, and I don't
know half of the procedures yet. I'll have to get on the
ball and study them if I expect to get up and down all in
one piece.*
    *From your letters I gather you have quite a variety
of experiences over at the U.S.O. I'm sorta envious of
you having something to do to keep you occupied. I'm so
damned sick and tired of this place that I'm just about
nuts. Every day or so a couple of W.A.S.P's fly in here and
we have a big time shooting the breeze with them. They're
the only females we've seen since we've been down here,
so you can imagine the kind of a play they get.*
    *Now Evaline Groves, you take care of yourself. You
oughta marry me so I could take care of you and vice
versa. That's my ambition you know and I'm looking
forward to it mucho! Love is a wonderful thing. Don't
you agree? Don't you believe that sex is an up and
coming thing, for business and pleasure etc. Oops, mark
out that last sentence, I forgot that we're not hitched yet
and I can't take any liberty with my thoughts and put
them into words. From now on, remind me to keep my
ideas and broad views to myself!*
    *About you coming down, baby, do you think you
can come down next week-end? I think that's around
the first of July. You could catch the same train outa
Nashville that I did, and you get into Birmingham
about 4:00 in the afternoon. We don't have to fly on
Sundays and if I can get a way up there, I'll be on my
way Saturday as soon as I finish flying. I can meet you
there Saturday evening but this idea won't work unless
I can get a car or get a ride up there. I'll write or wire or
maybe call you if I can get anything worked out.*
    *Well, Groves, gotta go now, I get to study how to fly
a P-40. If I don't learn it well enough, I may get washed
out or maybe—well, we won't talk about that. This is*

W-E-B-B signing off for the afternoon with, Love is where you find it and I found you! I love you, Evelyn. Cobby

Curtiss P-40 E

"Man! What an aeroplane. I was doing 400 m.p.h. today in a dive. It cruises about 225 and will do about 275 wide open straight and level. I sure was scared when I took it up for the first time, and when I got it in the air I was amazed how easy it was to fly and how little you had to remember as far as procedures go."
[Cobby Webb]

When World War II began, the P-40 was the best fighter available in the United States and served throughout the war by Allied air forces of 28 nations. Although often outclassed by adversaries in speed and maneuverability, the P-40 earned a reputation for extreme ruggedness.

June 30, 1944

Dearest Family.

I'm a little late with the mail this week but you know how things are. I've been flying a P-40.

Yesterday two other fellows and I sneaked over to Maxwell Field in our 40's and put on a little show over the field for the benefit of the single needle width boys they have over there taking B-24 transition, then we flew around until we found some 24's flying around, then we made passes at them, flew formation with them and even did barrel rolls around 'em—anything to make a nuisance of ourselves. We just about worried those poor guys to death. But from now on that kinda stuff is out. They caught eight guys in my section rat racing and dog fighting and they're going to be eliminated and maybe even court martialed.

No, Pop, I haven't gotten a lighter, nor a chain for my dog tags. I can't get a lighter anywhere, and I only wear my dog tags to fly in so there's really no need for a chain at the present. Give my regards to all and I'll try to write more often. All my love, Cobby

July 4, 1944

My Darling Evelyn,

As I sit over here on the flight line trying to study procedures, my mind keeps slipping off flying, and I find myself thinking about you. I keep thinking about how you looked at such and such time and I try to remember every little detail of the scene. In case you didn't know it, Baby, it was pretty darn hard for me to leave you last night. I didn't go to sleep for quite a while after I came back last night, and when I did finally drop off into slumber, I dreamed of you. Just can't get you off my mind! I sure am glad that you missed your bus yesterday afternoon, 'cause if you'd gone away feeling as sore at me as you were, I'd be worried to no end. As it is, I'm worried enough now, but not as much as I'd be if you'd left as sore at me as you were. To come right down to brass tacks, what I mean is I love you. I called the hotel this morning and you all had left. I guess you caught the bus to Birmingham. I hope you made a good connection all the way thru and didn't have to stand up any of the way.

Darling, I'm sure glad you came down here to see me. I sure am sorry that we had to have that little misunderstanding. I hope you've forgiven me. I honestly and truly didn't mean what I said. And you know I wouldn't intentionally hurt you for anything in the world. I was just P.O.'d at the whole world at the time and lost my temper. When you started talking like you did about severing relations with me—well, I just can't describe how terrible I felt—I felt about ten million times lower than a worm, and don't think I wasn't scared you were going to divorce me right on the spot. Remember, I'll love you forever, Cobby

P.S. Hey, sweetheart, you didn't lose your job because you didn't get back on time, did you? I hope not, but if you did, my offer still stands. You can have a permanent lifetime job with me anytime you want, just say the word, and you're "in like Flynn."

July 7, 1944

Dearest Family,

Sorry I've waited so long to write. We only got 7
hours in the P-40 because of the shortage of gasoline.
That P-40 is sure one whale of a good airplane. I sure
enjoyed flying it.

I wanta tell you about my first ride in the P-40.
Man, was I scared. I've never been so nervous and
flustered in all my life. I didn't breathe until after I had
gotten on the ground and had been there for about
an hour. The plane lands at 105 m.p.h and in case
you didn't know it, that's moving! And speaking of
moving, I did 400 m.p.h. in a dive. I lost ten thousand
feet before you could say spitfire. I couldn't even move
the stick to pull out, I had to pull out with trim tabs
and even then I blacked out for a few seconds. Lotta
fun, I really enjoy flying something hot!

We will pause now for station identification—this
is W-E-B-B, Craig Field, Selma, Ala. Buy war bonds &
stamps. "Back the Attack."

Yesterday the funniest thing happened. We were all
up in the tower shooting the breeze when we happened
to look out at a plane taking off. His tail had just lifted
off the ground, and the pilot, wanting to impress
people with showing them his prowess at the stick,
pulled up his wheels too soon, and because he hadn't
gotten up flying speed he skidded on his belly on the
runway for about two hundred yards. He stepped out
of the plane and stood there with a dazed expression
on his face. I'll bet he was the coldest hot pilot to ever
step foot in an airplane, but I'm not surprised 'cause he
was just a dull ferry pilot. Those guys have their heads
up and locked.

Evelyn came down Saturday. We had a swell
time. She was supposed to leave on the bus Sunday
afternoon, but she couldn't because it was so crowded,
so she had to wait over until Monday morning. That
made me very happy 'cause we had more time together.

As every day goes by, I realize more and more how
much I love that little ol' gal.

Well, day after tomorrow we leave for R.T.U. (Replacement Training Unit) in Tallahassee, Florida. I've been pretty busy today clearing post. I had to go get a bunch of signatures before I could leave and I still haven't gotten all of them yet. Tomorrow we're getting P.O.R.'d I don't know what it's all about, but whatever it is, it's a pain in the neck. But it has to be done before we leave post. We all have hopes of getting a furlough before long.

Gotta go to bed now, write soon. All my love,
Cobby

Replacement Training Depot
Dale Mabry Field, Tallahassee Florida
July 12, 1944

Cobby was sent to a Replacement Training Depot for a few weeks for ground school that prepared pilots for combat survival around the world. Soldiers who had returned from combat taught the classes. Cobby attended classes on how to survive a crash landing, how to treat and communicate with different cultures of people, practical tips for medical issues, and lectures on communication, radar, and secret intelligence. The goal was to teach pilots survival skills before sending them into combat.

July 12, 1944

My Darling Evelyn,

    Well, I'm finally here in ol' Tallahassee. What a town, it's just about like Selma. The field is pretty nice, though, and I think I'm going to enjoy my stay here. We're only going to be around for a couple of weeks and during that time we get 60 hours of ground school. After that we ship out to different fields around here where we start flying, and get our combat squadron together. They're telling us that we'll be going overseas within three months.

    I had a pretty good time in Montgomery Sat. night, before I had to catch my train down here. I ran into a whole mess of my buddies, whom I hadn't seen in months. 'Course a celebration was in order, and I'm not one to go against orders. My conscience bothered me until I remembered you were out to a big dance at the U.S.O. By the way, did you get the flowers in time to wear to the dance? I sent them with that intention.

    The trip down here was lousy. We had to change trains three times and not a bit of sleep was had by anyone. Ah, it was great.

    Listen Miss Groves, do you think that you may be able to get down here after I get down to R.T.U.? We may not be able to get home before we go over, and I damn well want to see you before I start ducking bullets. You know the married men down here live a life of Riley. They are allowed to live off the post, and they don't have to come out here until eight in the morning and get to leave by 5 in the afternoon at the latest. You know marriage has its good points. Sure wish I had a nice little wife to come home to after a hard day flying. But I guess that's out of the question.

    Well, sweetheart, I guess I'd better go, got to get an indoctrination lecture now. Write soon. I'll be seeing you. I love you, Cobby

July 15, 1944

Dearest Family,

I've been pretty busy getting settled down here. I figure I'll be here at the Replacement Depot for about two more weeks going to ground school five hours a day before being shipped out to a field. We have a fair chance of getting P-51's to fly, but the odds are in favor of P-40's. Personally, it doesn't make much difference to me, 'cause I know whatever I fly, it will be superior to the enemy's planes.

The ground school classes are really good, all taught by men who have returned from combat. And to give you an idea of what we're doing, we've been given lectures on survival after a crash up in the Arctic, jungle and desert and also how to act among the different classes of people in the combat theatres. Some of the lectures are about medicine, just practical things to do, in case of snake bite, diarrhea, dysentery, typhus, things that can be done to cure these ailments without the use of drugs or medical equipment, but by just using things nature has provided. We have had classes on communications, and they explain radar and some of the more secret radio devices that I can mention to no one and also lectures on combat intelligence and medical intelligence, telling us how they operate and what they do.

I sure wish I could go to a college where they have professors who know as much about their subjects as these boys, and who could present it as they can. I guess if the college professors got their training by practical experience as these guys did, it would make all the difference in the world.

I've been down here four days now and I haven't heard from Evelyn yet. I hope she's OK. She hasn't been too prompt in her letters lately, but she's probably busy, I hope. I sure was glad to talk to you. I wouldn't have called collect but I was a little low on dough. I got a $100 bond and gave Evelyn $40 for posterity. All my love, Cobby

July 15, 1944

My Darling Evelyn,
  First of all, I love you. Second, I'm pining away down here for you. Third, if I don't get to see you soon I think I'll either go nuts or desert or both! I've been down here for almost a week and I haven't received a letter from anyone yet. That's what I hate about changing stations. We never get mail for so long a time after we move. Takes over a week and just between you n' me I'm feeling pretty low, and my morale is about minus 100%. Low, huh?
  Well, baby, two weeks ago tonight I was a pretty excited kid. After all, my baby was coming to see me. Now I'm looking forward to another visit soon from my one and only, as soon as I'm sent out to an R.T.U., probably in a couple of weeks. Now, do you think that little trip could be arranged? I don't think I'll get another leave until after I get back from overseas, dammit all any how. If I don't get to see you before going to combat, I love you, and always will. You're a part of me that will only die when I do. And I hope you will wait for me until I come back.
  Some guy in my flight is a married man of exactly one week. He went home to Birmingham when we were delayed two days in route. Sunday, he was married and ten minutes after the ceremony, he was on the train to Tallahassee. No wedding night, no nothin'. He is only 19 and his wife is 17 and she's still in high school. She's going to summer school so she can finish. You know there is no love like a young love, I always say.
  I love you, Cobby

July 21, 1944

My Darling Evelyn,
　　First of all I want to tell you that I love you, and dammit don't you ever think any differently! If you do I guarantee you that I'll prove that I do.
　　Sure was glad to hear you talkin' last nite. I feel a lot better than I did. You sure sounded sweet. I just guess I'm gonna have to call you up more often!
　　We leave here in about a week, for R.T.U. down at Perry Field. That's about 50 miles south of here, and from what I gather it's pretty much of a no good town. It's the county seat of some county and all the town consists of is a chair. But I want you to come and see me even if you have to stay with me. Dernit, I sure wish I could get a leave, I'd sure give anything to see you and hold you in my arms. I've made up my mind for now and always, that I will never argue with you again if it is possible in any way. Now, of course, you will have to make some rules concerning yourself governing the gigantic impulse to argue with me. I believe with these ideas in effect, we can have a very satisfactory companionship, and that this most wonderful companionship will be considerably strengthened by merging our two separate lives into one of a blissful marital status. I hope that you whole heartedly agree with me on this tender subject. I want to confess that I have a notoriously nasty temper and I'll admit, for you (in case you won't, can't or do not have the urge to) that your sweet temper is equally and notoriously—NASTY! But that is beside the point. If I'm not careful, I'll be making ill concealed insinuations that will cause us to forget these two unusual resolutions even before they are incorporated.
　　I'm writing this letter in class, and you know as well as I that a person cannot do two things at the same time intelligently, so if this letter reads queer, have no qualms about my sanity. I'm trying to write this and listen to a very interesting lecture all at once. Before continuing this boring invective of my life at Dale Mabry, I would like to make a statement. If this letter

*is no good, at least it is dry and boring enough to put
a person to sleep just by reading it once. So if you are
suffering from insomnia may I recommend Dr. Webb's
superb and excruciatingly dry letters, guaranteed to
absolutely put you to sleep with one reading. If this isn't
true, we will cheerfully refund one canceled stamp. I
love you, Cobby*

July 22, 1944

Dearest Family,

I've been pretty busy lately going to ground school
five or six hours a day. We've been issued an oxygen
mask and flying helmets. We'll be leaving here for
R.T.U. in a few days, and we stay down there two or
three months, then back here and then P.O.E. It's
rumored pretty strongly that we'll be going to the
China-Burma-India theatre and that is a very logical
assumption because they have quite a few fighters in
England and then the Monsoon season is over about
October and that's when they'll probably start a big
push. The living conditions will be pretty rugged, but
I'd rather kill Japs. I hate the Japs more than anything.

I have hopes of getting home before going to a
P.O.E., but I don't know a thing about it. If they can let
us have a leave we'll get it but if they need pilots after
we come back from R.T.U., we'll probably go right
over. Speaking of R.T.U., I think I'm to be sent to Perry
Field about 50 miles south of here to fly P-40's, but in
all probability will get P-51's after we go overseas.

I gotta letter from Evaline, and she tells me she's
been feeling pretty bad lately. She fainted on the street
one day, and the doctor said she needed a lot of rest.
Her mother and dad had been away for a week and she
and her girlfriend had been keeping house, doing all
the cooking etc. I kinda believe that the trouble lies in

her cooking. Oh golly, if she can't take her own cookin'
what's going to happen to me when I have to eat it?

Evaline wants to come down when I get in R.T.U.
and I sure hope she can. I miss that lil' old gal like
mad. Everytime I think about us not getting married
right after graduation, I give myself a terrific mental
kick in the pants.

Mom, are you feeling OK? Now don't you worry
about me, 'cause I'm in perfectly good hands, and
anyhow the losses in combat are only about 5% in
fighter squadrons. So there is no worry on that count.

The chance of getting hit by an automobile in
peace time is almost as great as those of getting shot
down in combat. I gotta go now. All my love, Cobby

REFERENCES

1   "Winning Their Wings: Advanced Flying School." The Official Website
    of the National of the USAF. Accessed May 5, 2012. http://www.
    nationalmuseum.af.mil/ factsheets/factsheet.asp?id=1477.
2   North American T-6 Mosquito. The Official Website of the National
    Museum of the USAF. Accessed May 10, 2012. http://www.
    nationalmuseum.af.mil/factsheets/ factsheet. asp?id=287
3   "The Wings They Wore . . . Training Air Crews for WWII."Walnut Ridge
    Army Flying School Wings of Honor Museum. Accessed November 24,
    2012. http://www.wingsofhonor.org/Pages/wings.aspx.
4   Curtiss P-40 E Warhawk. The Official Website of the National Museum
    of the USAF. Accessed May 15, 2011. http://www.nationalmuseum.af.mil/
    factsheets/ factsheet.asp?id=478
5   "Forging Combat Pilots: Transition Training" The Official Website of the
    National Museum of the USAF. Accessed May 15, 2011.May 15, 2011
    from http://www.nationalmuseum.af.mil/factsheets/factsheet.asp?id=1677

CHAPTER NINE

Last Stop Before Going Overseas: Marriage, August 1944

Cobby is transferred to Perry Army Air Field, his last stop with Army Air Corps training before going into combat. During this four-month transition period, Cobby received final preparations for going overseas. He was assigned to train in a P-40 fighter bomber and would soon be traveling across the ocean to Europe to fight for freedom. His future was unknown, and Cobby was not sure when or if he would be coming home. But Cobby did know that he was madly in love with Evelyn, wanted to marry her, make love to her, live with her, and come home to his "wife" when the war was over.

August 5, 1944

Dear Family,
Well, I'm just getting settled down here at Perry. What a joint this place is. The field is completely surrounded by swamps, and there's nothing but scraggly pines and sand for scenery. There isn't a darn thing to do in the town of Perry. In fact, there isn't any town.

The only thing I like here is the food, and that's really been terrific so far. The nicest thing around here for miles is the Officers Club here on post.

Pop, I hope you get one of those lighters working 'cause I'm lost without one. I can't buy a lighter anywhere and I can't keep a dry match on me it's so hot down here. I am trying my darndest to get settled in this joint but I have to fumigate my bed every day to get rid of the bed bugs—quite a nuisance.

I hope to be seeing you all in a couple of months. Keep your fingers crossed. Incidentally, we're flying P-40's down here, and the ones we have are new ones and do they fly nice. Man! So smooth and easy. We'll probably get P-51's overseas because the P-51's are replacing the P-40's. Don't you all worry about me. I'm in perfectly good hands, the Army and the Lord's. All my love, Cobby

August 7, 1944

Hello Baby,

I know you're sore because I haven't written, but I've been terribly busy, and besides, I didn't like what you said about not coming down here to see me. Down here is your last chance to see me before I go over.

We're having a big argument up here at the Officers Club about the war and the Russians. So you can understand what a hard time I'm having writing this letter. I have a call in to Nashville, but the operator said it would take four or five hours to get the call through. If I don't call tonite, you know that it isn't my fault.

I've been flying quite a bit lately, got in three hours and a half today. Sometimes it gets so hot that you can hardly touch the planes, and then thunderheads come up so dern quick, that the field is closed in right down to the ground. Sometimes you have to land at another field 50 or 60 miles away and spend the night. It is a great life.

We got some more shots the day before yesterday, and it's all I can do to get around. I haven't hardly eaten anything, and I can hardly lift my arm. Oh well, such is the way of the Army.

Well, I don't guess that call is going to come thru before I have to hit the old sack. I'm about dead with fatigue. Oh yeah, I want to tell you about the time I had when I went horseback riding. I was in misery for about four days afterward. I had and still have a couple of blisters on my—we won't go in to where—and they were so sore I couldn't sit down, no kidding. I even had to sleep on my stomach. I've sworn off horses for good and that's no lie. If I'm ever caught on one of those four legged so and so's, I wish someone would take a little ol' gun and blow my little ol' brains out.

Now listen, Groves, you get yourself down here for about a week, and mind you I'm not taking no for an answer. Get that money outa the bank and put yourself on a train and come to Perry Fla. I'll be looking for you. Can't tell, maybe we'll get married. Oh my God, what am I saying, cross that remark off the books, hear???

Well darling, I gotta go to bed now, I have to get up early and fly in the morning. Write soon and remember I'm banking on you coming down but quick. All my love, Cobby

P.S. I heard from Mother, and she told me about one of my best friends getting hurt. He is a navigator on a B-24 and last week a couple ran together, he jumped but broke his back landing. He's progressing very well, although he'll have to wear a cast for 6 months. He's a swell guy too.

Evelyn responded to this letter with a weekend visit to see Cobby in Perry, August 19, 1944. Their weekend together was great, but too short.

I can only imagine the ride to the train station late Sunday night, August 21. It must have been agonizing to not only face another separation, but also to wonder if this would be the last time they would ever see each other. Cobby would soon go overseas, and many young soldiers were not returning home from the war.

As they were standing on the platform waiting for the train that would pull them apart again, Cobby started on Evelyn to stay with him and not return to Nashville. He remained persistent and persuasive about marriage, but I doubt it took much convincing as Evelyn knew in her heart that Cobby was the only man in the world for her. Love won out. Evelyn and Cobby were married at midnight by a notary public, and Cobby's high school ring was substituted as a temporary wedding band.

It was not as much fun explaining their elopement to both sets of parents who were surprised and disappointed at not being included.

"I'm a married man"

"My darling wife Mrs. Webb"

Evelyn's mother, Clarice, had hoped for a lovely church wedding for her only daughter, so in response to this news, she created a fantasy wedding that took place at Perry Air Field chapel, complete with a minister and family members who attended. This version of Cobby and Evelyn's wedding would be described in detail in the local newspaper. Meanwhile Fritzi, Cobby's mother, not as concerned about a planned wedding ceremony as she was about her new daughter-in-law making a "good impression" on the folks in the small town of St. Albans, fabricated a college education at Vanderbilt University in Nashville, Tennessee, knowing Evelyn had graduated a year before from a local high school there.

The following marriage announcement, written by the bride's mother, was printed in the Nashville *Tennessean* newspaper.

Miss Groves Becomes Bride of Dana Webb, Jr.

Mr. and Mrs. J.C. Lassiter announce the marriage of their daughter, Ruth Evelyn Groves to Dana Webb, Jr., Flight Officer, United States Army Air Forces, stationed at Perry Army Air Field, Fla., son of Mr. and Mrs. Dana Webb of St. Albans, West Virginia. The wedding was solemnized on August 21 at the Post Chapel of Perry Army Air Field. Only members of the two families and a few close friends were present. The bride wore an apple green linen suit, a white straw hat and white accessories. Her flowers were a shoulder bouquet of white orchids. Miss Myrtle Lougue of Perry, the bride's only attendant, wore a navy blue linen suit with a matching hat and accessories and a shoulder bouquet of gardenias. Stephen Stepanian, Lieutenant, United States Army Air Forces, stationed at Perry Air Field was best man. The bride was graduated from East Nashville High School. Mr. Webb was graduated from St. Albans High School, attended Greenbrier Military School and Miami University in Oxford, Ohio. He and his bride will make their home at Perry while he is stationed at the Perry Army Air Field.

The groom's mother, wrote the following marriage announcement that appeared in the St. Albans *Gazette*.

Of interest to their many friends is the announcement of the marriage of Miss Evelyn Groves to Flight Officer Dana A. Webb, Jr. which took place August 21st in Perry, Florida. The bride is the daughter of Mrs. J.C. Lassiter of Nashville, Tennessee, and the groom is the son of Mr. and Mrs. D.A. Webb of Ninth Street, St. Albans. The couple is at present residing at 501 East Bay St., Perry, Florida. The recent bride graduated from high school in Nashville and attended Vanderbilt University in that city. Flight Officer Webb is a graduate of St. Albans high school, attended Greenbrier Military School and was enrolled at Miami University, Oxford, Ohio when he was ordered to active duty in the Army Air Corps in February, 1943. He received his wings as a fighter pilot May 23rd, 1944 at Craig Field, Selma Ala and is at present taking combat training at Perry, Florida, preparing for overseas duty.

August 25, 1944

Dearest Family,

I guess you all want to know about my getting married. I guess you were pretty surprised 'cause I was surprised myself. We hadn't planned on getting married when Evelyn came down. But when she did come down, I realized I loved her too much to let her go back. We really didn't decide to get hitched until we

heard her train come in at the station here. We were married at 2401 hours August 21st. Evelyn says she's happy and I know I am. (But I sure did hate to break all those other girls' hearts!)

We have a pretty nice room out in town at a preacher's house. It really doesn't make much difference to me where we stay as long as we are together. She's going to stay here with me as long as I'm here. Her old boss back in Nashville told her she could have her old job back when I went over. Pretty lucky I'd say.

I'm getting along well down here with my flying. It's a lot of fun and very exciting. We do a lot of dog-fighting and rat-racing but don't worry because this is part of our training. When we dog-fight and fly simulated combat exercises we take pictures and they really look good when you see them. The instructors we have are really hot rocks. They've all been to combat and a few have victories to their credit. They are from all theatres. I've had a few funny experiences, like the day I went up on a high altitude mission to 25,000 feet and as I was going up my engine conked out on me. I was out over the gulf and I really started sweating. I kicked everything, pushed all I could get my hands on but she just wouldn't kick over. By that time I was down to 10,000 feet and I was all set to jump as soon as I reached 5,000 feet. Then I remembered that maybe I should change gas tanks. I did and she started purring like a contented kitten again. Talk about being relieved. My flying suit was wringing wet when I planted my number 10's on terra firma. I learned a lesson that day. And now when I'm flying those gas gauges in my ships are scrutinized every few minutes.

Boy, did Evelyn and I have a good time last night. We went to a cottage on the Gulf and had a big fish fry. Boy, what fish, they were the best I've eaten. It sure is beautiful on the Gulf at night with the moon shining. Evelyn and I sure got a big kick out of it. I'm up at the Officers Club with Evelyn now. If I'm lucky I think I'll get this finished. You know this letter represents about three days effort. I just haven't had enough time to finish it.

Say, how's Clate getting along? I bet he's big as a horse now at 175 pounds. That's quite a bit for my little brother. Oh pardon me, did I say "little" brother? I guess I'll have to drop that title of "little," huh? I knew he was going to be bigger than me, but I didn't think it would be so soon. I guess by now he is playing football and I bet he's a humdinger. I sure hope I get home to see him play. There's a good chance of getting a leave before going overseas.

I flew my first ground gunnery mission today, quite a bit of all night if you ask me. This was the first time I've ever fired with trace bullets. It's a lot easier, because you can tell when you're hitting the target. General Blackburn, commanding general of the third fighter command, was on the field today. The ol' booger flew in in the sweetest P-51 I've ever seen. It was brand new and only had about 20 hours on it.

Well, I gotta go for now. You all keep writing me like you have been. You've really been swell. Evelyn sends her best and will write you later. So long for now. All my love, Cobb

From this point forward, letters from Evelyn to Cobby's parents have been included to add a completeness to the couple's story.

August 30, 1944

Dearest Fritzi & Pop,

I'm really sorry that I haven't written sooner, but I've been kinda in a daze for the past week. I think it must be love!

I hope you all don't feel hard toward Cobby & I for not letting you know we were going to get married, but it was a surprise to us, too. In fact, I was at the train station getting ready to go back home when we decided to get married. I didn't know anybody could be so happy. I like very much being Mrs. D. A. Webb, Jr., and Cobby is so sweet to me.

We have a real nice room at the Baptist preacher's home. They are real nice to us. We've tried to find an apartment, but they just aren't to be found. Guess we'll have to be satisfied with a room. We were lucky to get that. Quite a few of the wives have had to go home because they couldn't find a place to stay.

You all should see the P-40's flying over. They are really beautiful. I looked inside one the other day and they have more darn gadgets in them. I don't see how a pilot knows what he's doing.

Well, guess I'd better close, as I've got to get dressed to go to the post. We eat there almost every night. It's real nice and the food is good.

Please write soon. All my love to my new mom & pop. Evelyn

September 2, 1944

Dearest Family,

I finally got a letter from you, Dad, today. It's been almost two weeks since I've been married and you didn't write me until now. I guess you don't approve of me getting married, but I'm sorry I didn't marry Evelyn sooner. We're so darn happy and our marriage is growing stronger every day. We were married by a Notary Public down here August 21st. We'll send you what her mother put in the paper and you can use it. O.K.?

I have about 35 hours now but today I'm on DNIF (duty not including flying). I have a pretty bad cold and the doc thinks that if I don't fly today that I'll be in pretty good shape tomorrow.

So Clayton is going to be a hot Rock in football this year, huh? Well, he's big enough. I sure wish I was there to give him a few pointers. But you be sure and tell him, DON'T be scared of those guys 'cause they put on their pants the same way he does. The harder you tackle or block an opposing player, the easier it will be on you. Now listen to me Clate, you might think this is a lot of bull, but believe me, this is straight stuff I've found by experience—the hard way. When you are tackled or blocked extra hard and you're pretty shaken, get up with a grin. Make the other guy think you like that. He'll lose confidence in himself and he will start missing you, and hitting you like a sack of cream puffs. Another thing, don't loaf around during practice. When you're running plays or having a dummy scrimmage, run hard, and put just a little more into it than the next guy. Play hard, put everything you have into the game. And you'll enjoy playing the greatest game in the world as much as I did.

I'm sure hoping that I'll get back there in about a month. I sure would enjoy a few good rounds of golf and watching the kid brother star in a couple of ball games.

Don't worry about Evie and I. We're very happy and very much in love with each other. Give my regards to all. All my love, Cobby

September 6, 1944

Dearest Fritzi & Pop,

Guess who? Yep, it's your new daughter again! We certainly did receive a sweet letter from you yesterday, Pop, and we certainly do appreciate, as well as need, advice. So anytime you feel like it, just send us more because we know we need it to start our new married life.

I'm enclosing a clipping of my wedding announcement that Mother had put in our newspaper. She "dressed" it up somewhat but at least it sounds good. So you can just have this announcement put in your paper if you want to. It has all the details & more, too.

Cobby had to fly last night until 12:00. I don't think he likes night flying very much. He says it's kinda boring. Lois' husband was going down the runway & didn't see a plane that was directly in front of him until he got right up to it. He turned his plane away from the other one, but his wings hit the other plane's wings and tore both of them up. Thank goodness, no one was hurt.

I've been pretty busy today. About 8:00 I went to Red Cross to roll bandages. I have joined the Officers' Wives Club and they have Red Cross every Friday. Well, after I finished that, I came home & washed out a few things and now it's almost time to get dressed for my favorite date. Guess who?

Mother & Daddy called me last night and they really did sound swell. This is the longest I've ever been away from them. I may go home for a few days next month.

Cobby and one of his buddies really had a good time yesterday. The two of them were flying together & a formation of Navy planes came over.

Cobby & Jimmy tried to fly formation with them,
but the Navy planes were just too slow. Cobby
said he would have had to put his flaps & wheels
down to slow up enough for them. They really
do have a lot of fun kidding about the Naval Air
Corps.
Well, I must close now as I have to IRON.
Isn't that awful? So until next time, love to all.
Lovingly, Evelyn

September 9, 1944

Dearest Family,

I've been late again on the mail, but the time
really slips by now that I'm a family man. Marriage is
a wonderful institution. Yep, Evelyn and I are really
happy.

I guess you are really enjoying the weather at home
now, but here it is as hot as July. I have heat rash all
over me, and Evelyn nearly goes crazy scratching my
back for me. I tried that heat powder you sent me,
Mom, but it only seems to spread it.

Well, we're the upper class here now and will be
through in about another month. I have about 45
hours in the P-40. Last week we had night flying.
Boy, was I scared when I took that plane up for the
first time at night. For the past week we've been
flying all day—gunnery missions, dogfights, low
altitude—everything. Let me tell you about the low
altitude cross country I was on this week. Six of us
were flying in close formation, the maximum altitude
was 200 feet, and when we were right on the gulf shore,
the altimeter read minus 100 feet. We had to pull
up for trees and high tension wires. I was flying my
instructor's wing when we saw a fire tower, we split, he
went on one side of it and me the other. We had to look

up to see the top. Boy, that was really fun. I'll bet half the cows in Florida gave sour milk that night!

Clayton, I hear you're having trouble with your blocking, not being able to keep your arm in. Now, if you'll concentrate on just keeping it in, you'll get in the habit of doing it in a few days. Also hold on to your jersey or pants or something that will remind you to keep it in. What has the coach got you playing, back or line? Whatever you play, don't ever forget that there are ten other men playing beside yourself, and the team that wins is the one that is best coordinated within itself. Always remember that if every man carries out his assignment, every play is a touchdown play. I hope to see you soon. Mother, don't work too hard! All my love, Cobby & Wife

September 16, 1944

Dearest Family,

I'm now on the flight line with a few minutes between flights. I just finished an aerial gunnery mission and I did pretty good. I got 42% and you only need 35% to qualify.

What do you all think about Joe Carter being in a hospital? I sure hope he isn't wounded too badly.

Hey, when you all write Evelyn, be sure to ask her how her bottom is. She went horseback riding the other day with a couple of other gals, and she could barely sit for a couple of days. I wasn't surprised. I learned by experience, and I kidded her all the time.

Oh yes, got some news for you. You know I told you I was only going to be here for two months and fly 81 hours? Well, the program has been changed, and instead of getting 81 hours, we're getting 120, which means an extra month down here. So I guess I won't get to come home until November instead of October, that is, if we get a leave at all. I'm not kicking a bit about that extra 40 hours 'cause it means an extra month in the states with my baby.

I've recuperated from the cold and am in fine shape. Evelyn is swell, too. We really have a good time together. I sure miss her during the day when I'm flying and in the evening, after I'm finished, I meet her at the Officers' Club where we have dinner together.

How's Clate getting along with his football? I'm expecting him to be an All American one of these days. You better tell that boy he'd better keep his nose clean and keep in condition.

The war situation sure looks good. The Allies went through France like a dose of salt. I hope they go thru Germany equally as fast. But I think the Germans will be pretty tough on the Deutschland. Well, I gotta go now. All my love, Cobby

September 26, 1944

Dearest Family,

Evelyn and I have moved. We have a much nicer room at a cheaper price.

Last Saturday a flight of 40's flew to Gainesville (Fla) and circled the Florida University stadium and watched the football game. Some of the guys around here will do anything.

We got up yesterday morning and were all set to go to church. Evelyn was all ready and waiting on me, and I had all of my clothes on except my trousers (I was putting on a fresh uniform). Well, I started to put them on and the zipper wouldn't come up. We worked for an hour or more on them, and when I finally fixed that zipper and put my pants on, I couldn't get the zipper open. Consequently, we didn't get to church, and I had a heck of a time getting my pants off. So I want you to know we were going to church, but circumstances beyond our control held us back.

I hope to be seeing you all in a couple of months.
All my love, Cobby

October 6, 1944

Dearest Family,

Sorry I haven't written sooner, but we've been
doing quite a bit of night flying, and I just didn't have
the time (stock excuse). We've flown five and six hours
a day for the past few days. I alone flew 18 hours in
four days, and that much flying really leaves me beat
out.

Pop, I took your advice and laid the law down
to the little woman. In fact, I not only insisted,
but demanded I receive a present from her on our
anniversary.

Evelyn and I bowled again last night, and she
almost beat me by getting a big 139, but I ended
up with a 157. But to hear her talk, you'd think she
bowled a 200 game. I guess that's what you'd call a
moral victory for her.

If nothing happens and the weather stays good,
we'll be heading out to sea to do a little fishing Sunday.
Evelyn is pretty excited, but scared to death that she'll
get sea sick. But if she takes your advice, Pop, and
sucks a lemon, she'll be OK, won't she?

Remember Stephen Stepanian, who was my best
man in our wedding? Well, he's in the hospital with
a badly dislocated shoulder. He was playing around
at Physical Training with a football. A bunch of the
fellows were each fighting for the ball to kick it. Step
caught it, then fumbled. He made a dive for the ball
and four other guys did also—at the same time. Step
ended up on the bottom and consequently, he's in the
hospital for 6 or 8 weeks. He misses shipping out with
us (all his buddies) and doesn't get to fly all that time.
This little story was for you, Clayton. I just want to

make you see the importance of not playing around. Over 90% of all football accidents happen playing sandlot ball without the proper equipment. Take heed, Clayton, and when you're on the football field either for practice or a game, get serious and stay that way. Don't play around or skylark, and you'll never get hurt!

Well, I gotta go now. I'll try and write again soon. All my love, Cobby

October 11, 1944

Dearest Fritzi & Pop,

First, I wanta tell you all how proud we are of Clayton that he's doing so well in football. Cobby read and re-read the clipping you sent. He was so proud of his little brother.

Well, our fishing trip didn't turn out so well. We left here about 5:00 Sunday morning and got down to the Gulf about 6:30 & had a good old country breakfast and got out to the boat around 7:15. It was a nice little boat. Had four bunks on it and was about 40 ft long. Just after we started, the darn gears broke on it & we didn't get going again until about 12:00. Oh, but we were disgusted! Finally, we started & went out about 30 miles & the weather started getting bad. Boy, did that boat rock. Cobby kept stuffing lemons down me & it didn't even bother him at all. He acted like an old sea dog, but I don't think I could ever join the Navy — they couldn't provide enough lemons. It was a cold day, and when we put the anchor down to fish, the darned old boat kept drifting. We didn't have a chance to do much fishing and finally got back about 7:00 PM. I sure was glad.

Well, I believe I've fallen in love all over again with my husband. He really is a sweet boy &

everybody around here really does like him. Pop,
ain't love grand? We only have about four more
weeks here, but I'm so glad we got married. I'll
never forget these two months.

Guess I'd better close. Write real soon! Loads
of love, Evaline

October 20, 1944

Dearest Family,
That hurricane heading our way has past.
Yesterday morning everyone was so excited. The
weather boys had led us to expect the hurricane in full
force at noon, but it veered to the east at Tampa and
went over the west coast and hit Jacksonville (directly
west of here 100 miles). It did quite a bit of damage to
Fla, 15-20 million bucks worth to the citrus crop alone.
Just glad it missed us. They vacated all the planes from
the field to Louisiana. I was supposed to go but I put
my foot down and said "No." I couldn't leave my little
wife here to face that ol' hurricane by herself. So they
took me off the flight.
Oh yeah, let me tell you about my flying a twin
engine plane. I went on a search mission Wednesday
to try and locate a bomber which had gone down in
the gulf (B-25) and I was co-pilot on a UC 78 about
the same as an AT-10. Boy, I sure am glad I'm a single
engine pilot. That plane handled like a ton of you
know what, and boring, my golly, I thought I was
going to go nuts! It was an experience, though. Now
I know what bomber pilots go thru—gotta give 'em
credit for having the patience to fly such stuff. We
didn't find the plane.
I think I will be leaving here about the first of
November. Sure hoping like mad that I'll get to come
home for a few days. I think they will give us at least

ten days. Don't know, though, the Army does some awful queer things sometimes.

Boy, St. Albans must have a terrific football team this year, beating Dunbar 46-6. I hope Clate doesn't let all his success go to his head. There is no bigger fool or chump than a conceited football player, so kid, don't let the size of your hat increase. Be confident in yourself, but never underestimate the other fellow.

Evelyn has finally finished dressing (about time I might say) so I guess we'll be on our way. We're going to mess (officers' mess) now, so I'll be seeing you (soon I hope). All my love, Cobby

October 25, 1944

Dearest Fritzi & Pop,

Well — we have at the most, 12 more days! Cobby has just about finished up with his 120 hours. He flew on Jake's (the captain that lives here) wing the other day & Jake said he really did stick with you & that's what a leader likes, so I believe our Cobby is pretty good. He isn't careless either, & I'm so glad. We've just gotta get a furlough, that's all there is to it! If we don't, we're going to be terribly disappointed, but I just feel like we will.

Our barn dance turned out super Saturday night. Everybody looked ridiculous. Cobby wore his old P-T pants, tied up with a rope, an old t-shirt, his old GI shoes, & carried a corn cob pipe. Oh, did he ever look funny! We just had oodles of fun!

The weather here has been beautiful since the hurricane, but it did a lot of damage. Outside of the orange crops being ruined, a shipyard was burned in Tampa. I'm glad it's all over with.

Mother keeps talking about the election at
home. It seems as if Roosevelt is THE man there.
Gee, I wish I could vote. The only trouble with Jake
is that he's a Republican & he's a nice guy, too! I
can't understand it. Lovingly, your rebel gal Evelyn

In November, Cobby finished flight training and received that two week furlough he had been waiting for so long. He and Evelyn traveled to St. Albans, West Virginia, where they spent time with his family and friends. While they were in St. Albans, President Franklin D. Roosevelt won his fourth term in office.

After two wonderful weeks with family, Evelyn returned to Nashville, Tennessee, to live with her parents, and Cobby returned to the base at Tallahassee to prepare for overseas duty. Saying goodbye, not knowing when or if they would see each other again, was a heartfelt pain that was difficult to bear.

November 22, 1944

Dearest Fritzi and Pop:
Well, here I sit all alone listening to Kay Kyser
[popular band leader and radio personality of the 1930s
and 40s]. Pooch, of course, is lying here by me, but
he's asleep and isn't keeping me company at all.
Golly, but I miss Cobby. It seems like my arm
or something is gone from me, but I know he'll be
back before very long, and we can take up where
we left off. I received a telegram from him a while
ago, and he's back in Tallahassee safe and sound.
He got reservations all the way back, and I fixed
him up with a box of fudge and some books. Hope
my fudge doesn't make him sick.

We certainly did have a wonderful time while we were with you all. Cobby and I were so happy to be there. Mother and Daddy want to go up to good old West Virginia over the Christmas holidays. I only get Christmas Eve and Christmas Day off. We're going to try real hard to get there.

Well—I started back to work today, and boy, is my new job hard! I have to keep books on all our new stocks and bonds and we have millions of dollars worth, so I'm gonna have to be very careful. Everything has to be checked over and over. I was real glad to be back at work though.

Has it snowed there yet? It's turning plenty cold here. Daddy has this house so hot though that I'm about to smother. Wait a minute—let me turn the register off.

Cobby and I had more fun coming back from Cincinnati. We had a whole section to ourselves and we slept part of the way, played cards, read, and just had the best old time. When we got home, Mother had us a nice dinner, and then we went to the show.

You all stay sweet & try not to worry too much about Cobby. I have faith in God and believe He'll bring him back to us. Write soon, Your lil gal, Evaline

November 24, 1944

Dearest Darling,

*You can't begin to imagine how much good hearing
your voice did me tonight. I was so blue until I talked
to you. Now I feel 100% better. When I left you it was
like leaving behind half of my soul. You're a part of me,
darling, a part that I will cherish forever. I love you,
Evelyn, more than you will ever know.*

*You know when I got on the train in Nashville I
shared a section with a civilian and he was griping
about the train ride. He'd been kicked off a plane and he
didn't like it a bit. You know I gotta little P.O.'d listening
to him gripe about all the inconveniences the war was
causing him, but I really blew my top when he said he
would be away from his wife until Dec 15. He said he
didn't see how he could stand it. It was at this point
when I went back to the lounge to have a smoke and to
also cool off. Can you imagine the nerve of that joker?*

*As you know I couldn't sleep coming down on
the train. I tried to, but I kept seeing you, the way
you looked as the train pulled out. And every time I
remembered something I said or did mean to you I
nearly died. Baby, when I come back I'm going to be the
sweetest guy you ever saw. I'm going to concentrate on
making you happy and keeping you that way.*

*Well, darling, it's getting late, and as you know
I'm an early riser. So I'll have to say goodbye for now.
I don't mean goodbye, I mean good night, sweetheart.
Don't worry and I'll be back with you in my arms before
you know it. I love you, darling. Cobby*

November 25, 1944

Hello Darling,

    Baby, you sure sounded sweet last night and I was more lonesome than ever after talking to you. You know, I'm kinda in love with you—strange isn't it, after all, you're just my wife. I still can't get used to referring to you as my wife.

    I wired you fifty bucks last night. I hope you got it OK. I also sent Dad the twenty I borrowed from him before I left home. I don't know when I'll get paid again, and then next month I won't get any flying pay, and with your allotment coming out, I doubt I'll have enough money to send.

    I tried to get you all some cigarettes, but they are being rationed from here, too. You can't buy Lucky's anywhere on the Field. I've been smoking anything I can get my hands on. Well, sweetheart, I gotta go now. I'll write often and you do the same—and darling remember I'll love you forever n' ever! Cobby

November 28, 1944

Hello Darling,

    How's my sweetheart today? Well, I'm still in Tallahassee, and I don't even know whether I'll leave tomorrow or not. I sure hope so. If I'd known I was going to be here this long, I sure would have brought you back with me. They could have given us a few days extra on our leaves without any trouble at all. Dernit all any hoo.

    Baby, I sure wish you were here, I'm lost without you. I don't do anything but read, play a little pool, and think about you all the time. I'd call you up every night, but it just makes me feel worse. Boy, when this war is over, I'm going to be the home-lovingest guy you've ever seen. I'm just going to sit around and make love to you, darling, and forget everything else.

If we go to the European theatre like I think we will, I should be home by next summer. That will really be swell! We'll spend a couple of weeks up in the mountains somewhere and just relax. What a wonderful thought.

What have you been doing besides staying home studying? What am I thinking of, I mean sewing and reading and going to movies and WHAT else do you do, sweetheart? Well, dearest I don't feel so well tonight, so I'll close for now. But Mrs. Webb, I want you to remember that I'll love you forever. Cobby

P. S. Don't worry, Honey, I'll be back before you know it.

December, 1944

Hello Darling,

Guess where I am?? On a boat out in the middle of the Atlantic somewhere. Personally I think the Captain is lost. I'm having a pretty hard time writing this cause it's pretty rough and the ship is pitching and rolling like mad. Now, I'll tell you something if you promise you won't tell anybody. Promise? O.K. Well I was a pretty seasick little boy the other day. Every time I got outa the sack everything went "round and round." I'm O.K. now, though the sea is rougher today than ever before, and I'm feeling fine as wine. I got my sea legs now. The reports from the war fronts sound pretty good tonight. The Japs are taking a pounding by 29's in Japan, and the U.S. Army, the boys with the feet, are knocking them over in the Philippines. They seem to be doing O.K. in the European theatre, especially in Germany.

We came through Philadelphia on the way up here. Gracie Allen and George Burns were on the platform in Philadelphia, and some of the guys got their autographs.

But they asked my buddies for their autographs in return.

Golly, sweetheart, I love you. I thought I'd better keep you informed on how I felt about you or you're liable to forget me and that would be disastrous. You know, Darling, if anything ever happened to you, or something came between us, I just don't think I could stand it.

Sweetheart, will you write Mom and Dad and tell them I'm O.K., feeling swell, with all the confidence in the world. Tell your Mother and Pop that I send my best to them and that we'll all be together in no time at all. In the meantime Darling, remember, I'll love you forever. Cobby

December 14, 1944

Hello My Darling,

I'm sitting here in my bunk reading your letters again, this only makes about the tenth time I've read them. I sure hope you and your folks get to go to West (By God) Virginia, for Christmas. I know that Mom and Dad will be awfully happy if you all did go there. This makes the second Christmas that I haven't been home. This one will be terrible, I know. I'm so lonely already that I don't know what to do. Thanksgiving dinner was a flop, it was terrible, and besides, I didn't feel like eating. I sure wish you had been there. Even bread and water would have been a successful Thanksgiving dinner.

I dream of you all the time, sweetheart. Sometimes when I dream of you at night I wake up and look around the bed for you, and when I realize where I am and that you're not with me, I feel awful. Just think, Darling, we've almost been married four months. The four months we've been married have been the happiest days I've ever known. And when I come *back, the following months will be even happier than the first three. Now listen, Evelyn, Sweet. I want you to be careful, don't neglect yourself, and if you get sick, don't you forget to go to the doctor. I'm serious, darling. I worry about you, falling down, getting hit by automobiles, getting sick—everything!*

Remember above everything, no matter what happens, I love you, Evelyn. Ever since I've known you, I've loved you. Now that we're married, I love you even more. I'll love you forever, Cobby

CHAPTER TEN

European Theatre of Operations, December 1944

At this time, the bloodiest war in history had been raging across Europe since September, 1939, with Americans involved since December, 1941. American airpower based in England involved the 8th Air Force that provided bombers and fighters, while the 9th Air Force performed tactical ground-attack and support missions. Strategically, bombers with escorts were used to hit Nazi industrial targets behind the front lines to slow war production while tactical airpower supported soldiers on the ground by attacking the enemy's frontlines. Both organizations had many bases in England, and thousands of airmen lived and worked there.

While Germany had experienced early success, the Allies' strategic air offensive against Germany began to attain its maximum effectiveness in 1944. The U.S. air forces had increased in numbers and improved in technical proficiency. Even more important was the arrival of the long range fighters, P-51 Mustangs, capable of operating at maximum bomber range. U.S. fighters could now get the better of the Luftwaffe in the air, while escorting the bombers deep into Germany. The P-51 had an extremely long range—enough to reach Berlin from England and return, with extra fuel tanks, and it was more than a match in speed and maneuverability for German fighters. As a result, the effectiveness of the bombers increased because fewer planes were lost or damaged, allowing them to fly at extreme ranges and mount massive attacks on the German oil production industries. By 1945, the unending Allied bombing and strafing raids on bridges, roads, railways, locomotives, and supply lines had paralyzed the German transportation system. Meanwhile, the Luftwaffe was dwindling as fighter plane production dropped and pilots were dying in aerial combat. The fight in the air contributed greatly to the victory of Allied air and ground forces in Europe. Overall the 8th Air Force alone destroyed 9,438 enemy aircraft and lost 3,000 fighters in the European Theatre of Operations.

The Allied forces fighting on the ground, by sea, and in the air throughout Europe were together pushing back enemy forces and advancing toward Berlin and the end of the war.

Cobby arrived in England before Christmas in 1944 and was assigned to the 328th Squadron, 352nd Fighter Group in Bodney England where he would fly a P-51 Mustang. The history of the 352nd Fighter Group, nicknamed the "Blue Nosed Bastards of Bodney," began in July 1943 and this squadron would become one of the most highly decorated USAAF

Fighter Groups in the 8th Air Force. Between 1943 and 1945, the 352nd Fighter Group would fly 420 missions, log 59,387 operational combat hours, and destroy 776 enemy aircraft.

December 15, 1944

My Darling Wife,
Well, I still can't tell you much, only that I'm somewhere in England. I had an English beer a while ago. I could compare the taste of it to something else but being you're a lady, I'll keep my mouth shut. What a time I'm having with English pounds and shillings. It's bad enough to drive a sober man to drinking. Can you imagine what it'll do to me?
I'm reading another of your letters again (#3), and I see you asked if I was being a good boy. Darling, I'm wearing a halo. I'll never think of another gal as long as I have you. Every time I close my eyes, I see you, yes, darling, no one but you. I think I love you more than anyone has ever been loved. That's a lot, and I want you to remember that always.
I'm living with Splitts and Gifford. It's not too bad. The room is pretty small, hell, small doesn't even describe it. You take one step inside and you can't turn around. But I don't mind, it's a heck of a lot better than some of the places I've seen and lived.
I gotta go now. Be careful, be good and remember as I said a few moments ago, I'll love you forever. Cobby

January 1, 1945

Hello Sweetheart,

Happy New Year!!! I'm down at R-28 in Furth [airfield in Germany] visiting Carl Weber, over the New Year. I've been here since Thursday [December 28] and everyone is asking me if I'm going to be stationed here permanently. That's how often I've been down here. We really floated the New Year in last night with a really terrific party. That is why I came down here. Those jokers at our field (R-29) don't have anything on their minds but Fräuleins. I get so damn disgusted with them I don't know what to do, so I come down here and leave them to their own devices.

I'm fine. I just can't make the days go any faster and God knows I try like mad. Give all my love to your mama and pappy and remember... I'm yours forever. Cobby.

January 9, 1945

My Darling Evelyn,

I received the first letter from you today since I've been in the E.T.O [European Theatre of Operations], #20, and I got up to #8 on the boat, so there's 11 lost somewhere between Nashville and England. I'm sure glad you liked the Xmas present you got from me, although I've never seen it. And about the breakfast set of dishes you got from your office, really a good deal. Now I wonder what we're going to eat the other two meals off of, the floor?

By the time you get this letter, you should have received $250.00 I sent this month besides your allotment. Yes, Darling, I know I shouldn't gamble but I only invested five pounds ($20), and see what I made? It's very cheap to live around here, so I'm going to send

you every bit I can afford. Put it in the ole sock, darling,
and when I get home we'll have something to start on.

Haven't been doing much here, as far as flying is
concerned because the weather is terrible. We have
about three inches of snow now, and it's still snowing.

Say Puddinhead, I do need something—you!!! And
nothing else. I'd be one unhappy so-and-so if I hadn't
married you. That's one big step I'll never regret, and
you can trust me to try my darndest that you will never
regret it either. Just be patient, my little wife, and I'll be
home before you know it, and we'll live like we've never
lived before!

Well Evelyn dearest, I must close now. Remember
whatever happens, I'll love you forever, Cobby

January 18, 1945

Dearest Family,

Well, I sure had a big day today as far as mail is
concerned. I got seven letters from home and seven
letters from my lil' honey. In regard to the length of
time it takes to get your letters, it varies quite a bit, like
today the earliest letter is dated Dec 3.

I just returned from London yesterday after
spending two days there. I didn't do much sightseeing,
I was too busy buying clothes at the PX. Only combat
personnel can buy stuff there and of course, we're
in that classification. I bought a battle jacket, really
looks sharp, too, and some other things like socks,
underwear and gloves etc. I walked down Piccadilly
and thru Piccadilly Circus. There sure are a lot of
people walking around and in the black-out, too. I
took a ride on the Tube (subway) to the suburbs. The
people are sleeping on bunks right there in the public
subways. No V-Bombs or Rockets hit London while I
was there, thank goodness.

I'm feeling fine, still don't have much time to my credit, but the weather is beginning to get a little better, so it won't be long till I'll be up there in the blue again. It sure is boring to sit on the ground all the time. In regard to the length of time it takes to get your letters, it varies quite a bit, from four to six weeks.

Say folks, I want you all to insist that Evelyn come and visit with you. I love her with all my heart, and I want her to be dear to you as she is to me. I'll never, as long as I live, ever regret marrying her. She has given something to me that I believe will make a better man of me.

So Evelyn gave you explicit instructions not to open your Christmas package. Suppose you write and ask her if she waited to open her presents. I'll bet 50 bucks she opened them as soon as they were received.

Say, did I tell you about the guy in my squadron (Lt. Emery Taylor) who bailed out over the lines, and on leaving his ship was knocked out. When he came to, he was hanging from his chute harness in the trees and he looked at his rip cord and it was still in the chute. As he fell through the trees, the limbs caught his chute and pulled the canopy out suspending him about 10 feet from the ground. He cut himself loose from the chute harness and ran like hell, thinking he was within the Jerry [nickname given to Germans by soldiers and civilians of the Allied nations] lines. He hid for about three hours until he saw a jeep with U.S. officers in it. He went up to them, told them what happened, they told him the forest he landed in was very heavily mined. The pilot damn near passed out at that! Quite a story, huh? Well I gotta go, give my regards to all, Cobby

"Lt. Emery Taylor. His chute didn't open, and he suffered minor bruises and abrasions." [Cobby Webb]

January 19, 1945

Army and Navy War Department, V-Mail Service

Dearest Family,
I haven't written in several days because I have moved to somewhere in Belgium. We're based at a little town, which the guys say is a typical French town, and I have a helluva time understanding what's being said, and how to make myself understood. I still haven't gone operational yet, dearest, and it may be a while. I guess by the time you've read this far, you'll know I'm not in England anymore. Our Group has been moved to Belgium, and that's all I can say, we're not very close to the front lines, so don't worry.
I hope this letter finds you all well and happy. I'm feeling fine, not working too hard, and enjoying myself just looking. The people in this section of

Belgium speak French and what a time we're having trying to talk to them. The people are very friendly and seem to think a lot of Americans. We're having a pretty tough time getting everything organized and settled.

All my love, Cobby

January 24, 1945

My Darling,

Well, today I am a man, yep, today I am twenty-one and am now a voter. Hooray, I'll get to vote for Frank in '48! I just came back from the club where I was celebrating this wonderful day with a few of the boys. Sure wish you were here.

We're listening to the Jerry [German] propagandist radio program. They're really beating out some hot jive, really get a kick out of those Nazis. Some of the crap they broadcast really isn't fit for print! Boy, I sure hope the Russians hurry and get to Berlin and do to all that get in their way the same thing that was done to them at Stalingrad when the Germans were trying to take Russia. Uncle Joe Stalin, my hero. Boy, I hope he keeps on hitting those Jerries with everything he's got up his sleeve, giving them all they deserve.

I haven't been doing much flying lately. The fog and bad weather have been terrible—we're socked in tighter'n a drum. Can't tell about this weather, tomorrow may dawn bright and sunshiny. Sure hope so. The less I fly, the more I want to.

I got the Varga Calendar [pin-up girls] you sent—thanks darling! I told the guys you sent it and they laughed and said, "what a broad-minded ol' lady you've got." Honey, do you know that I'm very lonesome for you right now, and all the time? Sometimes I wake up at night groping blindly around in my bed for you. I miss you more and more as each day goes by.

Well, my darling little wife, I love you and I guess I will as long as I live. Don't worry about me. Take care of yourself and remember we'll always belong to each other.
All my love, Cobby

The Battle at Stalingrad,
July 1942 to February 1943

Cobby referred to the Battle at Stalingrad as if it had just happened, although this battle had taken place two years earlier. At the time, the Soviet defenses topped the German advance into Russia and marked the turning of the tide of war in favor of the Allies. It was one of the bloodiest battles in the history of warfare with combined military and civilian casualties amounting to nearly two million.

January 31, 1945

Belgium

My Darling Evelyn,
Tonight is the same as last night, and the night before, and the night before that, etc. I've been thinking about you quite a bit lately, 24 hours a day, instead of the usual 23½ hours.
Quittenmeyer is lying on his sack singing the "trolley song" [Clang, clang, clang, went the trolley . . .] softly in my ear, so softly the windows are vibrating. Bob Ridge is writing a letter to his love. I've just talked him into getting married as soon as he gets home.
Well, let's see what I did today, got up at 0800 to go to briefing, but the mission was scrubbed, so at precisely 0807 I was back in the sack, dreaming of you,

*which incidentally was a continuation of the dream
I was having at 0749. Oh . . . it was nice. I'm going
to think about it all the time till I go to bed, so I can
start in where I left off when I woke up this morning.
I was dreaming of getting undressed to go to bed, and
if I continue the same dream tonight, well it oughta be
interesting. Don't you agree??*

*I just got back from mess, and it was pretty good
considering all of the confusion around here. But just
as soon as I finish writing this letter, I think I'll go
downtown and get some fresh eggs and chips, then I
won't have to get up for breakfast, unless we have a
mission scheduled.*

*One of these days I'm coming home, and from the
way Uncle Joe is going in East Prussia it might not be
long. I'm hoping to see you soon.*

*Remember, Evelyn, I love you body and soul and
you're in my every thought. Yours always, Cobby*

*P.S. Is your allotment coming through regularly?
You should have almost $500 by now.*

February 1, 1945

Hello Sweetheart,

*I got a whole mess of letters from you today and
also received the pictures you sent. I agree with you,
darling, they don't do you justice, but I don't need any
pictures to know how beautiful you are. So you kept all
those letters I wrote you while I was a cadet, huh! If I
didn't marry you, you were going to use those letters,
to sue me for breach of promise. I know, I should have
listened to Mother. She always said never to put one's
sentiments down on paper. Now I know she was right,
but alas too late. It's a good thing I loved you enough to
beg and plead, to have you for my wife. That's one thing
I'll never, as long as I live, be sorry for. I'm glad you're
glad, too.*

*I just got back from town where I enjoyed some
lovely eggs and French fries. Boy, when I get home
I'm going to keep you busy fixing up eggs and French
fries, and in your spare time we'll see what we can do
to contribute to the future generation. Does that sound
O.K. to you? Say yes—SAY YES! That's better.*

*I guess Mama Lassiter is having a helluva time
keeping you happy with stuff to eat. You always were the
eatinest gal I ever had the misfortune to buy dinner for.*

*Darling, I pine for you, dammit all any how, I'd
give a million dollars if I were with you this minute
(2310 Feb 1, 1945). You'll have to subtract five hours
to get that in Nashville time. Try and remember and be
sure to write and tell me where you were and what you
were doing at this time.*

*Say honey, in your letter tonight, you said
something about "our night" in the park, when I was at
the Classification Center. Do you still remember that?
If I remember correctly, that was where I first told you
I loved you. Am I right? That's been a long time ago,
but I can remember it like it was yesterday. That was
the last night we were ever there alone. I don't believe
you exactly trusted me, and you were probably right as
usual. As you know, I always was a sexy lil ol' booger.*

*Oh, did I tell you I've started smoking a pipe? Cigs
are scarce here and incidentally, I'd like to have a few
cans of Sir Walter Raleigh or Half and Half. Think
you can arrange it? Thank you very much, Mrs. Webb.
Merci Beaucoup.*

*Well, darling, I must close for now. All my bloody
roomies are crying about getting the lights out for
tonight, so Au Revoir for now, sweetheart. I'll love you
always, Cobby*

*P.S. Voulez-vous coucher avec moi? [Would you like
to sleep with me?] Don't slap my face when you translate
this. You're the only one I'll ever ask this of.*

The 352nd fighter group had been moved to the air base in Chievres, Belgium, to prepare for combat operations. From 1940 to1944 this air base was occupied by Germany until the Allies liberated it in the fall of 1944. The 352nd Fighter Group soon got into action flying numerous missions that included downing enemy planes, escorting bombers, and strafing targets on the ground. In total, during the month of February 1945, the 352nd Fighter Group conducted 17 missions over enemy territory, with 34 missions conducted in March. An important mission took place on March 24, 1945, in support of U.S. troops crossing the Rhine into Germany.

"By golly, I'm flying a P-51, the fastest fighter plane made! She's the best in the ETO" [Cobby Webb]

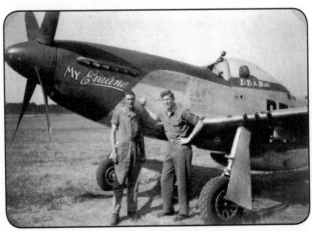

"My crew chief Sgt. Wagner and I with My Evaline" [Cobby Webb]

"The 328th on Y-29 in Belgium"

"Major George Preddy, 328th C.O. was shot down and killed by our own ack-ack December 25, 1944. Preddy was a leading ace in the E.T.O. with 33 aircraft destroyed." [Cobby Webb]

"Col. Jim Mayden, Lt. Col. Willie Jackson, Maj. George Preddy, Col. Joel Mason, Lt Col. J.C. Meyer. The big wheels at 352nd" [Cobby Webb]

"We're getting ready to take off . . ." [Cobby Webb]

"Give 'er the gun" *[Cobby Webb]*

"A 250 pound frag bomb exploded under the P-47 on landing. The pilot walked away." *[Cobby Webb]*

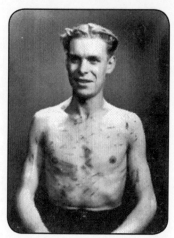

"Gestapo torture" with cigar and cigarette burns" *[Cobby Webb]*

"Col. Webster presented the Distinguished Flying Cross medals to Lt. Bill Reese, Capt. Vitek, Col. Mayden, and Capt. Bostrum." The Flying Cross Award was given for extraordinary achievement and heroism in aerial flight. [Cobby Webb]

"Hot Rock"

February 5, 1945

My Darling Evelyn,
    I'm still in Belgium, and it reminds me a lot of the gentle hills in West Virginia. I hate to disillusion you, but I doubt I'll be home for quite a while 'cause we have to get 300 combat hours and the weather has not been cooperating, so it may take a long time. The only thing I'm counting on is the discontinuation of the war. If the Russians keep going—well, you can never tell.

I went on a liberty run last night to a pretty good sized town around here, with the intention of getting stewed, but I found out that drinks cost around 2 bucks a throw. That ol' stuff ain't no good, so I drank beer, which is very mild. I tried drinking some cognac but it curled my hair, so never touch it. They say it will make you go blind if you drink enough of it.

Darling, thanks a lot for the birthday cards. I only hope that on my 22nd birthday I'll be home and will celebrate with a big blow out. I was trying to get you some lacy unmentionables, but no soap. If I get to Paris, I'll see what I can do. I must close now, gotta hit the sack, I'll be in the blue tomorrow if the weather breaks. Remember, Evelyn, I love you more than words can tell. Cobby

February 8, 1945

Hello Sweetheart,
The weather is bad today, as usual, so I'm going to write you now instead of tonight.
We're just getting things set up over here. We have steam-heated barracks which are pretty nice, and there are only three or four in a room. We're sleeping on army cots, but as soon as our supplies get to us, we'll have nice hospital beds with mattresses. We have our quarters fixed up pretty good now. We have a nice big closet made out of belly tank boxes and have our clothes hung up again for a change. The food here isn't worth a dern, but it is expected to improve as soon as things become a little more organized, either that or a few cooks are going to lose their stripes. We've been eating C rations ever since I've been here, and C rations aren't what I call filling. I'm always hungry and if you could send me a nice box of candy, nuts and anything else to eat, I'd be very happy. I'd sure like that Evie Webb special fudge, I

can almost taste it now, and you ought to send me some cigars and pipe tobacco.

Say, honey, how are you getting along? I'm feeling fine, only hungry. I sure hope you get to go to W. Va. Soon. They want you to come and see them in the worst way.

In your last letter you said something about you were going to love me to death when I get home. I'm sure looking forward to the time I can have you in my arms, and feel your lips against mine, um, sure could do with a little loving from you right this minute.

I'm having a terrible time trying to learn this damn French. But maybe by the time I get home I can carry on a lil' conversation. Well, dearest, I gotta go now, it's eatin' time and although the meals are lousy, I can't afford to miss any. So until next time, I'll sign off. I'll love you always, Cobby

February 15, 1945

My Darling,

I've just returned from a mission, and I'm pretty tired, so I will try and write a coherent letter, but you'll have to be the judge of that. It was a good day's work if I may say so, 5 and a half hours worth, which is the most work I've done since I've been flying. It was interesting, and don't think I wasn't scared. I've never seen so many planes in the sky at one time, and all of them ours. The Jerries must be hoarding their planes and pilots for one last great try. Even the flak was moderate, even light. I was flying the Group CO's wing and we really had a time coming home, strafing a train, but luckily there were no heavy ack ack guns around. The weather is still pretty bad around here but I expect it to break pretty soon, and when it does, the Jerries have had it.

Gotta letter from Mother the other day telling me about the death of a friend of mine who was a gunner

on a B-17 in Italy. I'm sure glad I'm flying fighters.
I wouldn't give two cents for all the Bombers in the
E.T.O. There is a new replacement in my squadron by
the name of Petty. He knew Hancock, the boy who was
killed in P-40, at advanced.

These Belgium people are O.K. I like them, on a
whole, much more than I liked the Limeys [English].
You should hear some of the stories they have to tell
about when the Jerries were here. Most of them were in
the Maquis [guerrilla bands of the French Resistance] or
in the Underground and a few were in hiding from the
Germans because the Jerries were going to send them to
a work camp. Some of the stories make your hair stand
on end. Also I saw some collaborationists in town the
other day. They were all women who had their heads
shaved, and their hair is just now coming in again.
They're all social outcasts and most of them are watched
all the time. They are shown no consideration at all,
either by civilians or the Army. But then, that's been too
good for them.

I'll be glad when this war is over and you're back
in my arms again. I believe I love you more than it is
possible for normal human beings to love each other.
Give my love to your folks. I'll love you always, Cobby

Although familiar with the French Underground Movement in Europe during World War II, Cobby's exposure to "maquis" and "collaborationists" prompted further research. The French Underground Movement started after France surrendered to Germany in 1940 and signed the Armistice agreement that gave Nazi Germany control over and occupation of three-fifths of this country. At that time the Gestapo began hunting down communists and socialists living in France. France had already surrendered all Jews living in France to Germany and disbanded the French army of 1.5 million soldiers, sending them to prisoner of war camps.

Thousands of French patriots and soldiers fled to the forests of the unoccupied zones to hide. These men and women gradually organized into groups, better known as the "Maquis," a French word for small scrub bushes used for cover against the Germans. These groups bravely defied Nazi authority through sabotage and espionage. Some of their activities included intercepting military messages, spying on the enemy, publishing anti-fascist newspapers, cutting phone lines, de-railing trains, destroying bridges, hiding Allied airmen from capture. They found many ways to resist the Nazi occupation. The contributions made by these brave ordinary French citizens, hunted down by the Nazis, contributed greatly to their country and the war effort. The French patriots had no tolerance for the group of traitors referred to as "collaborationists." These French men and women "collaborated" with Germany in many ways after France's surrender. When France received liberation from the Allies, some collaborationists were convicted of war crimes and those women who were suspected of having romantic liaisons with Nazis, were publicly humiliated by having their heads shaved.

February 18, 1945

My Darling Wife,
    I guess you're about ready to knock my head off for not writing you as much as I should. I don't blame you a bit, sweetheart. I know just how you feel when the mailman doesn't visit you often. But truthfully, darling, I've been pretty busy. Our squadron is now in the middle of building a pilots' room out on the line, and between flying and building, I'm so tired at night, all I can do is fall in bed.
    Yesterday was a big day for me. I went on a high altitude escort job, and we were gone over five hours. I really was tired when I got back. It was a lotta fun though, even if I was scared and excited. Well, I only have 294 hours and 40 minutes to go and I'll be thru. That's the day I am looking forward to.
    Say, that's a good deal about Berry Field closing down. Maybe we can get some of those chairborne soldiers [those with desk jobs] over here to do a lil' fightin' for a change. Especially those Paddle feet [slang: an Air Force personnel member who lacks distinctive rating

and is occupied with ground duties]. *You know I never did like those so and so's. Not even when I was a cadet. We have some over here at our field, but they're all pretty good Joe's. Not like those in the states who try to run everything.*

Say kid, what's this I hear about you getting a raise?? Tell ya what I'll do, if you learn to cook, by golly, I'll give you a raise, too!! Instead of kissing you once when I kiss you, I'll kiss you twice. Hey, what am I talking about? I'll be getting the raise, not you. Just guess I'll have to think of something else. Say Evelyn, I didn't know that you could sew. My gosh, you sure do keep your talents to yourself. Remember the time at Perry, when I kept pestering you to sew a button on my pants, and you kept forgetting? But I think you finally sewed it on when I threatened to do it myself.

Dearest, I'd give ten years' pay to see you sitting in this room grinning at me. By Darn, if this war isn't over soon, I guess I'll just have to go A.W.O.L. and hitchhike back to the states. Just think, Evelyn, in two more days we will have been married six months. I just wish that I could have been with you all of that time instead of just half of it. Darling, I can hardly believe that it's you talking, when you say you want to raise a football team. Are you sure no one hit you in the head with an addin' machine?? I just hope I'm as much a man as you think I am. After all, I'm just a weak lil' ol' pilot, not Superman. But I'd sure like to give it a try.

Well, darling, the intelligence officer just came in and said we have briefing in a few minutes, so I'll be on my way. Remember darling, you're always in my heart. Love you forever, Cobby

February 21, 1945

Hello My Darling,
How are you 'bout now? I'm fine, but pretty lonely
these days. I'm supposed to be on pass now, but I don't
feel like goin' out gallavantin' around. Besides I'm a lil'
low on the green stuff.
I got the snapshot and you look kinda young, baby,
and I think that short skirt becomes you. You know, I
always did say you had the best looking legs of any girl,
and that still goes!
Did you know that today is our six months
anniversary? Just think, you've been my wife for 183
days. That doesn't look like a very long time but these
past few months have seemed like centuries to me. I'll
sure be glad when I can hold you in my arms again and
whisper in your ear that I love you with all my heart.
Darling, the very thought of you is all that keeps me
going sometime.
So you're having trouble getting cigs. Well, baby,
you're not alone. I've been sweatin' out butts for damn
near two weeks, been smoking any and everything I
can get my hands on. Even German cigars, which are
nothing but dried cabbage leaves. Even been smoking
cigarette butts in my pipe!
The weather over here is beginning to break, and I
don't think it will be long until spring will surround us
with all its glory. Remember, darling, you're always in
my heart. Love you forever, Cobby

February 25, 1945

Dearest Family,
I was so glad to hear that you all liked my in-laws
(crudely put) and that their visit was enjoyed by all. I
was kinda afraid that there might be a flurry of fists
and feet, and maybe a lil' hair pulling, when two sets

of hillbillies sat down to eat. Did anyone receive any serious hand injuries by fork jabs, when the pork chop platter hit the table?? I sure wish I could have been there. Maybe it won't be too long until I get home, now that the U.S. is on the move. In a few weeks the German officers on the front lines will be giving the command "About face, fire!" "About face, fire!" That's the day I'm looking forward to.

Too bad about J.E. Payne getting wounded. He must have been in the thick of it.

Went on my second mission yesterday, and a grand time was had by all. But I do not wish you were here. Well folks, I gotta end this bull session now as us pilots gotta get our beauty sleep. Wings alone are not enough to keep a wife happy. So long for now. Write often and so will I. All my love, Cobby

"I'm set to go." [Cobby Webb]

A day in the life of an escort fighter pilot, as described on the National Museum of the US Air Force website.

Weather plays a huge factor in fighter and bomber operations and is quite complicated without sophisticated radar available. Each base has a team of weather officers who, every hour, record cloud conditions, wind speed and direction, air pressure, and temperature to make a forecast. Since weather in England tends to be cloudy, there are long periods of weather too poor to fly in with much visibility.

- The day begins about 4 a.m. with a quick wash and shave, dressing, and breakfast of powdered eggs.
- Flyers then gather for a briefing on the day's mission—assigned rendezvous with the bombers, expected enemy defenses, determine if the weather is good enough to fly and so on. If all systems are on go, we set our watches together and head for the field in trucks.
- It's easiest to write your engine start time on your hand with the identification letters of the plane you're supposed to follow on take-off. As soon as our group is airborne we form up and head for a rendezvous with other fighter groups and bomber formations before crossing into enemy territory.
- With the long range of the P-51's we can escort the bombers to and from the target. Our primary job is to stick close to the bombers and protect them, but we also go after German fighters and ground targets such as freight and group trains.
- Returning to base, we leave our planes and go directly to an intelligence briefing and report how many enemy aircraft we had seen, with details of time, place, altitude, and direction. Then we recount the facts of aerial combat, weather, and what we had seen on the ground—truck convoys, ships, troops or other important observations.
- After the de-briefing, flyers usually check the roster for the next day and watch the gun-camera film from the day before, followed by a brief rest, dinner at the mess hall, and a stop at the officers' club for a nightcap before bed.

The 8th and 9th Air Force organizations had many bases in England with large numbers of American airmen living and working to keep fighter planes in the air—jobs like maintenance, engineering, weather, firefighting, food service, medical, photographic, administration, police, intelligence, and many other operational functions. On the flightline, each fighter had a ground crew that made sure aircraft were ready to fly each mission, and they were backed up by hangar crews, propeller and engine mechanics, painters, electricians, carpenters, and maintenance teams.

In the air, a typical fighter group used 48 aircraft in three squadrons of 16 fighters each. Squadrons were divided into four flights of four. Two aircraft—a leader and a wingman—formed an element, the most basic fighting unit. On most escort missions, a few spare fighters followed the group to replace anyone who had to turn back before entering hostile territory.

Fighter formations changed according to mission needs, but general principles always applied. A formation had to be organized and controllable. On escort missions, fighter groups arranged themselves above, in front of, and to each side of their bombers, with still more fighters out in the direction of the sun to forestall attacks difficult to see because of the sun's glare. Fighters tried to stay with their bombers to fend off the Luftwaffe, but as the Allies gained control of the sky, they were able to chase enemy fighters and attack ground targets.

February 26, 1945

Hello Darling,

Just a short note before I hit the sack, telling you how much I love you. I got three letters from you today, all dated in January. One in particular interested me. You sounded sorta P.O.'d at me, baby, because I hadn't been writing you all the time. Honey, don't worry, when you don't hear from me, it isn't because I don't love you, because you know that I do, with all my heart. Our life around here is pretty irregular and things don't come off exactly as planned. So believe me when I say I'm pretty busy. I try to write you as much as possible, because I know you like to get mail, just like I do. But sometimes I just can't do it.

So you want a baby, huh, Sweetheart? Reading your letter reminded me of a poem I read today:

<u>*Little Willie*</u>

When Willie was a little boy
Not more than five or six,
Right constantly did he annoy
His mother with his tricks.
Not yet a picayune cared I

For what he did or said
Unless, as happened frequently
The rascal wet the bed.

Closely he cuddled up to me
And put his hands in mine,
Till all at once I seemed to be
Afloat in seas of urine.
Strong odors clogged the air,
And filled my soul with dread
Yet I could only grin and bear
When Willie wet the bed.

Tis many times that rascal has
Soaked all the bedclothes through,
Whereat I'd feebly light the gas
And wonder what to do.
Yet there he'd lie, so peaceful like,
God bless his curly head.
I quite forgave the little tyke
For wetting of the bed.

Ah me, those happy days have flown;
My boy's a father too,
And little Willies of his own
Do what he used to do.
And I! Ah, all that's left of me
Is dreams of pleasures fled;
Our boys ain't what they used to be
When Willie wet the bed.

Had I my choice, no shapely dame
Should share my couch with me,
No amorous jade of tarnished fame,
No wench of high degree;
But I should choose and choose again
The little curly head
Who cuddled close beside me when
He used to wet the bed.
—E. Field

How da'ya like that, sweetheart? Well, I have to close now. Remember I'm thinking of you always, and look forward to the day when I'll get to catch up on all that back lovin' that you're saving for me. You're pretty smart catching up on all your sleep now, cause you never spoke truer words when you said you "didn't think you'd be doing much sleeping when I get home." I love you, Cobby

March 2, 1945

Hello Sweetheart,
Another month has gone by and that's one less month I'll have over here before I can get back to you. I hope you're OK. As for me I have a pretty bad cold and haven't been flying for a couple of days. Today our group shot down seven planes and here I was sitting on the ground.
Darling, I wish you wouldn't say that I hurt you when you don't hear from me. It makes me feel like I'm neglecting you. I write whenever I have time, and you must realize I have a lot to do besides fly. I have to read and study lots of dope that may save my life sometime.
Say honey, you know I have only received one package from you since I've been over here and that was your pictures. I can't understand it. I've only received one from home, too. I'm still hungry and would like anything you can send to eat and I'd like a pipe and tobacco.
I think I'll go to Brussels this week-end and see if I can buy something you might like for your birthday. Maybe next year you'll be celebrating your twenty-first birthday all snuggled up in my arms, mmm... what a nice thought. All my love, Cobby

March 10, 1945

Dearest Family,
   I've just returned from a short visit over Germany.
Things were quiet, and no action whatsoever. Gets
mighty boring when there is nothing to do except fly
straight and level. I'm sorry I haven't written, but I've
been pretty busy, getting Hitler down on his knees. I've
had a pretty bad cold lately and that has caused many
complications in my flying schedule. I have about
twenty or twenty five hours to my credit now which is
the equivalent of five or six missions.
   Went into Brussels last week on a two day
pass. I spent all my money and didn't get anything
worthwhile except a couple of pair of hose for Evelyn.
I'll bet those hose are the most expensive hose she's
ever worn. They cost about 15 bucks a pair—'course
they're black market stuff and that's what hikes the
price way up.
   I sure was sorry to hear about Bill Bartlett getting
killed in Italy. But that's the way things go. Gene
Wietzel is OK, isn't he? He'll be coming home pretty
soon, huh?? All I can say is fighters are the safest plane
to fly in aerial combat, especially if they're P-51's doing
high altitude escort work.
   I guess by the time you get this letter my press
notices will have been printed in the Gazette. I was in
on a strafing show. Well, I gotta go now, it's chow time.
All my love, Cobby

Flight Officer Webb Receives Award

St Albans Gazette, 1945

An Eighth Air Force Fighter, Flight Officer Dana A. Webb Jr., of St. Albans, recently shared with his group commander and a third P-51 Mustang pilot in destroying a locomotive and in damaging eight flat cars loaded with German war articles in the area of Meiningen, Germany.

F/O Webb flies a Mustang in the high-scoring 352nd Fighter Group, which has destroyed more than 650 enemy aircraft, both in the air and on the ground. The group recently received the coveted War Department's Distinguished Unit Citation "for extraordinary heroism, determination and esprit de corps in action against the enemy" during a bomber escort mission to Brunswick, Germany, when the 352nd shot down at least 2 enemy aircraft. On a subsequent mission with 38 Nazi planes in the air, F/O Dana's squadron accounted for 24 of that total, a record for an individual squadron in the European Theatre of Operations.

F/O Webb was graduated from St.Albans High School in 1941, and spent one year at Greenbrier Academy. After one semester at Miami University, Oxford, Ohio, he joined the Army Air Forces.

His wife, Mrs. Ruth Evelyn Webb lives in Nashville, Tennessee, while his parents, Mr. and Mrs. Dana A. Webb, Sr. live in St. Albans.

March 13, 1945

Hello Darling,
 I've just come from the flight line. I was looking over my missions and I have a total of twenty-five hours. Been pretty busy lately, getting our room fixed up and flying. I like this base better than the one back in England. We have a nice set-up. The only gripe I have is that we're starving to death. We're still eating C-rations and it doesn't look like much chance for a let up any time soon.
 I still haven't received any of the packages you've sent except the pictures. I can't understand what's holding up the mail, unless some of these jokers are stealing the packages and selling the contents to the black market, which flourishes very openly over here. In fact, that is the only place you can get anything. A pack of cigarettes cost you a buck and a half and all clothing is really expensive. I paid about six dollars for a scarf that you could buy at home for a dollar. I'm having a helluva time stretching my pay from one month to the next.
 I haven't received any mail from you for several days now. I got to thinking maybe you're kinda P.O.'d at me for not writing, and decided not to write just to get even. Darling, I know I haven't been very good about writing these past few weeks, but you know how busy I've been. After a mission I can't do anything but hit the sack. I'm really exhausted after four or five hours in the air. We're not flying today so I have time to write letters.
 By the time you receive this letter, your birthday gift will or should have reached you. I hope you like what I got and I hope they're small enough. You know I haven't had much experience with that type of goods. Which reminds me, I haven't told you in this letter yet, so I'll tell you now. I guess I'm more in love with you than Romeo was with Juliet!

Well, the schedule was just posted for tomorrow's mission. It's one of those early morning jobs and I'm on it. So I'll close for now, Baby, and try to get a good night's sleep, but I never do before a mission. Write soon. All my love forever, Cobby

P.S. Send me something good to eat and a red or white scarf (please).

March 28, 1945

Dearest Family,

As you have probably read in the newspapers during the last few days, we've been pretty busy over here. The weather has been superb. We can see all the way to the Russian lines, and as a result, Germany has really taken a pasting. We've been flying two missions a day, and getting up in the wee small hours, and in some instances making pre-dawn takeoffs.

I had a shot at my first Jerry pilot the other day. He was flying a jet job. I only had time for a snap shot at him, and he was gone. Chased him, but he pulled right away from us. We were only doing 500 mph.

Spring is wonderful. I'd almost say that spring in Belgium is almost as pretty as spring in good ol' West (By God) Virginia. Well, finally, the packages you all have sent me are starting to arrive. I received one with 12 pks of Luckies, and some cookies and date bars. Really did appreciate the swell eats and the smokes. One thing about food over here, and that is you can never get enough of it. The St. Albans Gazette is coming pretty good and I've received about all the issues in Feb. Day before yesterday I sure did have a pleasant surprise at mail call, a nice fat letter from St. Albans with lots of pictures, and I really think that they're terrific! Mother, you n' Dad are growing younger by the day! I'll be derned if Clate doesn't look like the side of a barn and well, Clate, I guess you're glad that basketball season is over—now you can really concentrate on the women. I know that you carry a club around with you all the time to beat the women off. That's the way I usta do. (I tell everyone.) But now that lil rebel gal occupies my thoughts.

I'm sure glad J. E. Payne is OK and back in the states. I guess that boy really has some stories to tell. Give him my best, and when ol' Gene gets home, be sure and tell him I asked about him. The same goes for Bob Dillon.

Say, don't let anyone kid you on the mail situation. Air Mail is just as fast as V-Mail, and lots of time, faster. I get letters from the states now in about two weeks.

I got a nice letter from Lee asking about Evy and telling me how he was doing in the Navy. He said that he'd been recommended for flight training. Hope he makes it OK. Can't beat flying, I always say. You all know I never was one much for walking. But I'll have you understand that all isn't a bed of roses. Especially sitting for five hours in a cramped position at thirty thousand feet on a dull escort mission. But when back sitting on the ground, batting the breeze, talking planes and experiences, you get a sense of importance and you say to some pilot next to you who hasn't gone operational yet, "There I was, thirty thousand feet on my back, over Berlin, with flak bursts all around, and my engine quits!" And the other fellow looks at you with big eyes and asks "then"? You laugh and say "Oh I just switched over to a full gas tank and started breathing again."

Well, I guess I'd better sign off for tonight. It's past my bedtime. I'll write again as soon as time permits. All my love, Cobby

April 1, 1945

Darling,

Things over here are pretty lively about now,
with Patton going thru Germany like a dose of salts. I
guess you know by now that the Ruhr Valley is almost
completely surrounded by the British and Americans.
I'm afraid that people are going to get optimistic again
and that's the worse thing that anybody can do. I believe
that Germany will fight to the last inch of their country,
and I'll bet they have a few tricks up their sleeves.

Today is Easter Sunday. The weather here has been
pretty bad all day, a pretty gloomy Easter. I went to
church this morning but couldn't keep my mind on the
sermon. I was thinking of you constantly, Evelyn. This
is the lonesomest I've ever been in my life. Four months
away from you seems like forty years. But the way the
war's going, it looks like I may be home before you know
it.

I got the pictures you sent, baby, and I really like
them. You know you get prettier and prettier every day.
Well, young lady, how does it feel to be twenty years
old. I'll bet you don't feel a bit different. I wish I could
have been there to give you twenty licks and three for
good health. But I will make a point to do that as soon
as I get back to you. I'm sure glad you received the hose.
I was sweating them out and sorry they were too big. I
don't know much about that kind of stuff, so you'll have
to forgive me this time.

I got a few letters from home a few days ago, and
from what they say, everyone is swell. Dad started his
garden on the first day of Spring, and I guess he has
Clayton down there sweating with a hoe in his hand.
I'm sure glad Pop didn't have the garden bug when I was
Clayton's age. I can just see me plowing corn.

Give your Mom and Dad all my love and tell them I
hope to enjoy their company very soon. I guess I'd better
close now. I'll love you forever, Cobby

The "garden bug" was part of a national movement and war effort that went on across the country. Evelyn's family also had a garden, as families were encouraged to grow "Victory Gardens" to help overcome wartime food shortages and to have more food available for American soldiers. One estimate was that the gardens accounted for forty percent of the country's total vegetable harvest during the war years.

April 3, 1945

Hello Darling,
Today has been a pretty busy day for me. First thing this morning, Quittenmeyer, VanderVeen, and I went to the Eighth Fighter Command headquarters and met the board to become second LT's. We all passed, it was nothing but a formality, and we will receive our commissions in a week or so. After returning from there, we went out to the Squadron Ready room to see if we were wanted for anything, and there I found out I had been awarded the Air Medal, which I will send to you as soon as possible. When you get it, I'm going to ask you to send it home so Dad can have a look at it, but be sure to have him send it back to you, because I want you to have that, Darling. The weather around here is regular April weather, so we haven't been going on too many missions. I'm scheduled to fly tomorrow, and if the mission goes off as planned, it will push my time up to about seventy combat hours.
Our lines are within 180 miles of Berlin tonight, and I expect this war to rapidly draw to a head in the next couple of weeks. Keep your fingers crossed, honey. It won't be long now!
Oh yes, baby, I got another package from you yesterday, one with caramels and jelly, also cigs and a couple of packs of pipe tobacco. Thank you very much, sweetheart.
Darling, do you remember the night in the park where I first told you that I loved you? I can remember

it like it was yesterday. That was the night I told myself that you were going to be my wife. Boy, am I glad I was right! I love you with all my heart, Evelyn, and I'm just trying my darndest to fly as much as possible so I can get back to you. Always yours, Cobby

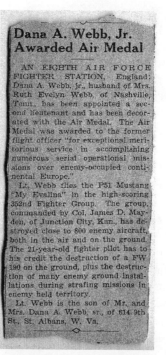

Dana A. Webb, Jr. Awarded Air Medal

AN EIGHTH AIR FORCE FIGHTER STATION, England: Dana A. Webb, jr., husband of Mrs. Ruth Evelyn Webb, of Nashville, Tenn., has been appointed a second lieutenant and has been decorated with the Air Medal. The Air Medal was awarded to the former flight officer "for exceptional meritorious service in accomplishing numerous aerial operational missions over enemy-occupied continental Europe."

Lt. Webb flies the P51 Mustang "My Evalina" in the high-scoring 352nd Fighter Group. The group, commanded by Col. James D. Mayden, of Junction City, Kan., has destroyed close to 800 enemy aircraft, both in the air and on the ground. The 21-year-old fighter pilot has to his credit the destruction of a FW 190 on the ground, plus the destruction of many enemy ground installations during strafing missions in enemy held territory.

Lt. Webb is the son of Mr. and Mrs. Dana A. Webb, sr., of 614 9th St., St. Albans, W. Va.

Dana. A. Webb, Jr. Awarded Air Medal

AN EIGHTH AIR FORCE FIGHTER STATION, England: Dana A. Webb, Jr., husband of Mrs. Ruth Evelyn Webb of Nashville, Tenn., has been appointed a second lieutenant and has been decorated with the Air Medal. The Air Medal was awarded to the former flight officer "for exceptional meritorious service in accomplishing numerous serial operational missions over enemy-occupied continental Europe."

Lt. Webb flies the P-51 Mustang "My Evaline" in the high-scoring 352nd Fighter Group. The group, commanded by Col. James D. Mayden, of Junction City, Kan., has destroyed close to 800 enemy aircraft, both in the air and on the ground. The 21-year-old fighter pilot has to his credit the destruction of an FW 190 on the ground, plus the destruction of many enemy ground installations during strafing missions in enemy held territory.

Lt. Webb is the son of Mr. and Mrs. Dana A. Webb, Sr. of 614 9th St., St. Albans, W.Va.

April 10, 1945

Dearest Family,

I have a few minutes before briefing, so I'm going to try and write this letter. As you've read in the papers, no doubt, you know that we've been pretty busy over here. We've flown all over Germany and still the Luftwaffe sits on the ground. On my first mission, I got an ME 109 on the ground. Our group got forty on the ground that day, and the next day got sixty-six on another field. Just like shooting fish in a barrel, and no flak to speak of and no aerial opposition whatsoever. They did come up the next day though and 90 of them were shot down by the Eighth Air Force.

Did you know the closest distance between the Americans and Russians is less than an hour's flight in a 51? I personally don't see how those Krauts can last much longer.

I have almost eighty hours combat time now, and I'm just about due for a cluster to my air medal. I told you I got the Air Medal, didn't I? I've sent it to Evelyn, with instructions for her to send it to you all so you can get a look at it.

The weather here is wonderful. It's almost like May in the States. You just can't ask for better flying weather. Write soon. All my love, Cobby

April 11, 1945

My Darling Evelyn,

Spring is here and a young man's fancy turns to love, and here I am 2500 miles away from you, Baby. I'm going nuts.

We've been pretty busy the past week, really been working the Reich over, Kiel one day, Berlin the next and so on down the line. I have better than eighty hours now, would sure like to get a hundred right quick. I didn't tell you about being in the flight that knocked down an ME 109 the other day, did I? He passed right under me and if I hadn't been so surprised I could have gotten in a shot at him. As it was, the flight leader got on his tail and drove right up his blind spot shooting all the time till the pilot hit the silk [parachuted].

Gosh, Evelyn, isn't it terrible that President Roosevelt died. Boy, when I heard that, I damn near fell over. I couldn't believe it. I just hope that Truman fills his shoes half as well. And then today, Ernie Pyle killed in action. I don't know what to say.

Evelyn dearest, when you write home, tell the folks I'm O.K. and not to worry. Gosh, it seems like years since I saw you last. Keep loving me darling and always remember, no matter what happens, I'll love you forever. Cobby

President Franklin D. Roosevelt Dies
1882-1945

Franklin D. Roosevelt, nicknamed "FDR," was President of the United States from 1933 to 1945, holding this office for four consecutive terms. Faced with the Great Depression and World War II, President Roosevelt guided America through its greatest domestic crisis, with the exception of the Civil War, and its greatest foreign crisis. By 1945, the United States had become a global power with global responsibilities and in April of that year President Roosevelt, in declining health, visited his favorite retreat in Warm Springs, Georgia, for a much-needed rest. During this stay he collapsed and died unexpectedly on April 12. The world was stunned. Hundreds of thousands of people, many with tears in their eyes, lined the train route carrying his body from Georgia to Washington, D.C., and then on to Hyde Park, to pay their final respects.

Losing President Roosevelt before the war had ended in Europe or in the Pacific was surely unsettling for America's citizens and our Allies abroad. America's new president, Harry S. Truman, was sworn in that evening. The next day he told reporters, "When they told me what happened yesterday, I felt like the moon, the stars, and all the planets had fallen on me."

President Truman faced unprecedented and defining challenges in foreign affairs during the first year of his presidency. However, the United States, with its newfound political, economic, and moral leadership, would play a leading role in shaping the remainder of the twentieth century.

Ernie Pyle

Ernie Pyle was a popular American journalist during World War II who wrote from the perspective of the soldier. He won a Pulitzer Prize in 1944 and was killed in an attack by the Japanese on an island off Okinawa April 18, 1945.

April 18, 1945

Dearest Pop, Fritzi & Clate,
Sure was glad to get your sweet letter today. I was getting mighty anxious for one!
Oh — I had a letter from Cobby about two days ago, and it was written on April 3rd. He'd just been informed that he had become a 2nd Lieutenant and had been awarded the Air Medal. Goodness — I'm so proud of him!
Guess you all read in the paper where the Air Force had shot down over 3,000 planes. It said that Germany had only a few left & the ones they did have couldn't be flown because of lack of fuel and pilots. It just seems that it can't go on much longer over there.
Wasn't it terrible about Roosevelt? Honestly — around this house and every other house in town practically — it was just like somebody in your own family had died. I hope & pray Truman can lead us through this war. He's gonna need the support of everybody, though. And it sure was a bad thing about Ernie Pyle, too. I loved his columns.
It just came over the radio that 9 Russian armies are entering Berlin. It said that Berlin was in flames. I refuse to get optimistic, though. Well, I must get to work, so you all write real soon! All my love, Evaline

April 25, 1945

Dearest Family,
I guess you all are kinda wondering why I haven't written. Well, we just returned to England from Belgium and with the confusion of moving and getting set up here, and all the while flying missions, I haven't

had time. I have flown in 25 missions and have about 110 combat hours now, so I'm thinking I won't be getting much more in this theatre. The missions we have now are nothing but milk runs—we're only in Germany anywhere from thirty minutes to an hour. Combat flying in Europe is just about finished. I have high hopes of going to the states before heading for another theatre, but you know the army. Anything can happen.

I sure am sorry to hear about J. E. Payne being in such a bad mental condition. He sure must have seen a lot of rough action. I should think that rest and relaxation would fix him up pretty quick.

I hope this letter finds you all well and happy. I'm fine, and you needn't worry at all.

That fishing deal sounds mighty good from these parts, sitting on the bank in the shade really appeals to me. You don't think I'm getting old, do you? Just think, a pipe and slipper man before I'm twenty-two. Now, it could be laziness.

All my love, Cobby

April 28, 1945

England

My Darling Evelyn,
    How's my baby tonight? Fine, I hope. I'm O.K. but beginning to get a little bored with all the inactivity. We haven't flown but about two or three missions in the last two weeks. I hear there just isn't hardly any place left to bomb in Germany.
    Well, honey, your ol' man finally got out of the enlisted status. Yep, as of today I am a 2nd Looie. Now, I'm sweating out my 1st which should be coming along in a couple or three weeks. I must confess that I've had plenty of time to write, but with my promotion I've been buying drinks every night, with all the guys I know being treated by me, as is the custom with new promotions. And of course with every round I buy, I have to have one myself. Last night everybody in the squadron was soused. Here I am going around breaking up fights, when the first thing I knew, I was almost in one myself. After that I came home and went to bed.
    I guess you know by now that the Russians, Americans and British have all joined forces. The Russians have Berlin surrounded and have pushed 45 miles to the west of it. I'm thinking the European War is all over. Well, gotta go now darling, it's sack time. I'll sure be glad when I get home to sack up dual again with you. I'll love you always, dear, Cobby

2nd Lt. Dana A. Webb Took Part in Assault

AN EIGHTH AIR FORCE STATION, ENGLAND. 2nd Lt. Dana A. Webb of St. Albans, W.Va., who took part in the air assault against Germany has been decorated with an Oak Leaf Cluster to the Air Medal for meritorious achievement during sustained combat operations over enemy territory. A cluster signifies an additional award of the same decoration.

Lt. Webb, who set fire to an FW 190 shortly before the VE Day, flew against the enemy as a member of the 328th Mustang Squadron, which is part of the high-scoring 352nd Fighter Group. The three squadrons in the group accounted for almost 800 Luftwaffe planes, both in the air and on the ground, between September, 1943 and the end of hostilities. The group, which holds the Distinguished Unit Citation is commanded by Col. James D. Mayden, of Junction City, Kansas. [*Article in unknown paper, 1945.*]

REFERENCES

1   WWII Nissen Hut. The Official Website of the National Museum of the USAF. Accessed July 15, 2012. http://www.nationalmuseum.af.mil/ factsheets/factsheet.asp?id=923

2   352nd Fighter Group: History." The Official Website of the Eighth Air Force Historical Society. Accessed September 15, 2012. http://www.8thafhs.org/ fighter/352fg.htm

3   North American P-51D Mustang. The Official Website of the National Museum of the USAF. Accessed September 15, 2012. http://www. nationalmuseum.af.mil /factsheets/factsheet.asp?id=513

4   Reese, B. & Wilson, B. 2008. *The Last Reunion—A Gathering of Heroes—Chapter 1.* Front Runner and Split S Productions. Accessed

November 24, 2011from http://www.snagfilms.com/films/title/last_reunion

5   "The 352nd Fighter Group History." Official website of the 352nd Fighter Group Association. Accessed September 15, 2012. http://www.352ndfightergroup.com/ assoc/main.html.

6   "Captain George E Preddy." The Official Website of the Preddy Memorial Foundation. Accessed February 22, 2013. http://www.preddy-foundation.org

7   "Distinguished Flying Cross." WW2 awards.com website. Accessed January 22, 2013. http://www.ww2awards.com/award/241

8   "Battle of Stalingrad." The History Channel Website. Accessed September 26, 2012. http://www.history.com/topics/battle-of-stalingrad

9   International Museum of the Air Base of Chièvres, Belgium. Accessed December 26, 2012. http://www.warmuseums.net/Pages/belgium_mu_detailed39.html

10 "Maquis". The Spartacus Educational Website. Accessed September 28, 2012. http://www.spartacus.schoolnet.co.uk/FRmaquis.htm.

11 "WWII, French Resistance: European Theatre." The Beyond Curricula Website. Accessed September 30, 2012. http://www.beyondcurricula.com/wwii/europeantheater/resistance.html

12 "Tennessee 4 Me, The Great Depression and World War II, Life on the Homefront." Tennessee State Museum. Accessed July 10, 2012. http://www.tn4me.org/ minor_cat.cfm/minor_id/71/major_id/9/era_id/7

13 "Roosevelt Facts and Figures: World War II." The Official Franklin D. Roosevelt Presidential Library and Museum Website. Accessed September 15, 2012. http://www.fdrlibrary.marist.edu/facts.html#wwii

14 "American President, Franklin Delano Roosevelt: A Life in Brief." Miller Center at the University of Virginia Website. Accessed September 15, 2012. http://millercenter.org/president/fdroosevelt/essays/biography/1.

15 "Ernie Pyle Is Killed on Ie Island; Foe Fired When All Seemed Safe." The New York Times on the Web Learning Network. Accessed December 27, 2012. http://www.nytimes.com/learning/general/onthisday/bday/0803.html

16 "Combat Chronology of the US Army Air Forces, April 1945." United States Army Air Forces in World War II. Accessed March 25, 2013. http://www.usaaf.net/chron/45/apr45.htm

CHAPTER ELEVEN

Victory in Europe, May 7, 1945

By the end of April 1945, the Americans with Western Allies and Soviet armies had advanced into the heart of Germany and surrounded the enemy from all directions. The 8th and 9th Air Force had achieved air supremacy over Germany with their bomber and fighter planes, and the Luftwaffe had been reduced to catastrophic levels. Strategic bombing and air attacks on rail systems made transportation of war material difficult, and the successful air attacks on the oil industry halted production and manufacturing of oil needed, crippling the German war industry. The ground forces of four million men, two thirds of them American, and the Soviet armies with nearly seven million soldiers were controlling Germany city by city. As the Allies moved through Germany, they discovered tens of thousands of concentration camp prisoners. Many of the prisoners suffered from starvation and disease. Other locations were identified that had been used by the Nazis to imprison and exterminate an estimated eleven million people, six million of whom were Jews. The world was stunned to learn of the unfathomable moral disaster that had taken place in Germany.

As the war in Europe was coming to an end, the two dictators of the Axis powers, Benito Mussolini of Italy and Adolf Hitler of Germany, were dead. On April 28, Benito Mussolini, while attempting to flee from Italy to Switzerland with a convoy of German trucks, was captured by a group of Italian anti-Fascists Partisans and executed by a firing squad. His body was taken to Milan and hung for public display in one of the main squares of the city.

Two days later, April 30, as the Battle of Berlin raged around him, Adolf Hitler realized that all was lost, and not wishing to suffer Mussolini's fate, the German dictator committed suicide, along with Eva Braun, his long-term mistress whom he had married less than forty hours before their deaths.

On May 7, 1945 Germany surrendered unconditionally to the Western Allies and the Soviet Union, and the war in Europe was finally over! It had been a long five years and eight months of bloodshed and destruction, with a large population of people homeless, starving, grieving, and in despair. Rebuilding Europe and finding peace would not be easy.

The New York Times

Tuesday, May 8 1945

VE-Day

THE WAR IN EUROPE IS ENDED!

SURRENDER IS UNCONDITION-
AL; V-E WILL BE PROCLAIMED TO-
DAY!

Reims, France, May 7—Germany
surrendered unconditionally to the
Western Allies and the Soviet Union
at 2:41 AM French time today. [This
was at 8:41 PM, Eastern Wartime
Sunday.] The surrender took place
at a little red school house that was
the headquarters of Gen. Dwight D.
Eisenhower. Germany surrendered
with an appeal to the victors for
mercy toward the German people
and armed forces.[48]

May 9, 1945

My Darling Evelyn,
I guess on V-E day plus one you must be plumb
tuckered out. Likewise!! Only I'm afraid I gotta head
start on you, being we've been off ops for over a week
now and we've been celebrating the fall of Germany ever
since then. Evy, sweet, I gotta admit I've been stewed
to the gills every night during this hilarious celebration
period. But last night took the cake. Capt. Poltrack
(my roommate) and I got lit pretty early, about dark,
on drinks which were on the house. So we decided we'd
have a little fire works, so off we go up to the control
tower and steal a couple of flare guns and a couple of

hundred flares and started shooting them off. Boy, were they pretty. Then the tower officers came up, and we all started shooting off rockets, magnesium flares and everything we had, but to top everything, some guys in another squadron got themselves some flare pistols and some flares and we had a regular war. Shooting flares at each other at about a hundred yards range from behind the barracks. You could see them coming in plenty of time to duck, so it wasn't too dangerous.

For the past week there's been a party on the base constantly and everyone has been blotto. Colonels, majors, all the wheels hobnobbin with all the junior spokes like me. Whiskey sure is a social equalizer.

We're still sweating out leaving jolly old England. No one knows what we're going to do or when. I'm just hoping like hell that we'll get to go home before we go to the Pacific. The way things look now we're going to be here for quite a while before we go anywhere.

Darling, have I told you lately how much I love you? I haven't? Well, I am now, sweet, you mean more to me than you'll ever know; I miss you so much, that half the time I don't know what I'm doing because I'm constantly thinking of you. The other night I had the most horrible nightmare. I dreamed you didn't love me anymore and I woke up in a cold sweat with a firm resolution of never again eating sardines and pickles before I go to bed, as long as I live. I love you and how I need you, all my life!!

Now that the weather is improving, I think I'll take a short trip down to London on my next pass. I think I'll go and see if London is as lighted up as New York at night.

I told you about the custom on this base, about having a crap game the night after payday, didn't I? Well, as you might guess, I got into it this month and was pretty lucky, so you oughta be getting a couple of checks soon, $250 total. Take a hundred for new duds and sock the rest.

Baby, how's Momma and Pappy? You be darn sure to tell them I sent all my love and I don't mean perhaps. You tell Momma that I can taste that ol' southern fried chicken way over here. Loving you and eating fried

chicken are going to be my main interests as soon as I
get home. 'Course I could live on love alone, but that's a
rich diet.

Well, dearest Ev, I guess I'd better close now. I feel
much better having written you. It's almost as if you
were here and I was talking to you. If only I could put
down on paper how I love you and how much I need
you, all my life!! Maybe I wouldn't have that tight
choked feeling I have inside of me now with my heart
almost bursting with love for you. Always remember,
Evelyn, I love you, and only you, you're all that I'll ever
want and I can't wait until I have you in my arms again.
Always Yours Evy . . . Always. Cobby

May 11, 1945

VE +3

England

My Darling Sweetheart,
These last two days have been very fruitful for me
as far as mail is concerned. I've received 5 letters from
you. All of them make my heart ache with loneliness. If
I don't see you soon, Evelyn, I don't know what the hell
I'm going to do.

Sorry you were let down by the peace rumors
in April, but you didn't have long to wait until the
European war was finished. Boy, England is really
jumping, from all reports. I've done all my V-E day
celebrating right here on the base. So I only know what
I hear.

This meal that you cooked up, tell me, sweet, was
it really good??? You better do a lot of brushing up on
your culinary arts 'cause I mean to test you out when
I return from the war. I've been thinking about what
we'll do on that delayed honeymoon of ours. I'll tell you

what I've planned, and you can tell me what you think. I'd like to go home, get the car from Pop and go up in the mountains. It's just about a hundred miles from home and it's really beautiful. There is a small lake up there and we could rent a cottage and stay there all by ourselves for about a week. There's only one draw back. It's quite a resort in the summer and it may be a little crowded for our tastes. Truthfully, I don't give a damn where we go as long as I'm with you, so darling, decide what you want and we'll do whatever you want to do.

I love you, I love you, I love you, I love you, I love you, I love you, I adore you my most dear and beloved wife. Yes, Dear, I must admit I like black gowns and pink ones, too, and lacey ones, and sheer silk ones, there ain't no doubt about it, I like all gowns, just so they're on you!!

Well, today we had another big softball game and we won, of course. We haven't lost a game in the league so far. I think that's pretty good don't you? Yesterday we scraped the infield, and what a job. We had to borrow (polite word) a tractor and we found a snow plow and drug it all over the field until it's as smooth as a billiard table.

Above all, remember I love you with all my heart.
Cobby

May 16, 1945

Dearest Fritzi, Pop & Clate;
Thought I'd better sit right down & write you all a letter to let you know that I heard from that man yesterday! It was written on May 9th & he was in such good spirits. It was the longest letter that he'd ever written to me (6 pages). I nearly fell over. He said that they had really been happy & excited over the fall of Germany. I was so relieved to get his letter 'cause it's been over a week since

I'd heard a word & I was getting worried. I can understand, though, why he doesn't write more. I think it's much easier for us here at home to write, 'cause we do have a little variety in our lives, but when he gets home & after he's been here for about twenty years, I'm really gonna jump on him for not writing more while he was away.

Oh yes, Cobby sent me a picture of "My Evaline." It's just the prettiest plane that I've ever seen. Oh well—just stop & think what a good looking pilot it has.

Mother canned some cherries the other day & they are wonderful! She says she's gonna can every vegetable she can get her hands on. Fritzi, we can't get any meat around here either. It's a good thing we like vegetables. Oh, what I'd give for a great big thick steak! Pop, I hope your garden is doing okay. When I come up there, I'll help you work in it.

Well, I must close now & get to work. If I hear anything else I'll let you know. Sure will be glad when next month comes 'cause I really wanta see you all! Bye for now. Lots of love, Evelyn

May 24, 1945

Dearest Family,

I've forgotten how long it has been since I last wrote but I know that it has been way too long. I'm terribly sorry but with the excitement and celebration of V-E day, it's been busy. I've just returned from a seven day "flak" leave in London. I had quite a good time there, saw quite a few interesting sights and several good plays. I saw changing of the guard at Buckingham Palace, which is quite colorful, but not like pre-war days. I stood around outside the Palace for a couple of hours once, but I still didn't get to see the King or Queen.

Well, things are beginning to pick up over here now. It's just like being in the training command again, with ground school and training flights. Oh me, and I was so looking forward to taking it easy. I guess the big wheels want to keep us busy, so we won't get stale, until they decide what to do with us. I hear a new rumor every day. The latest is we're going back to the states and train in jets. But don't be surprised to get a letter postmarked "Iwo Jimo" one of these days. Oh yes, now it can be told where I am in England and where I was in Belgium, since censorship has been lifted. I'm at Bodney Airfield in England, East Anglia about 50 or 60 miles due west of Yarmouth and about 100 miles north of London. In Belgium we were stationed about 50 miles southwest of Brussels in a place called Mons, almost due west of Liege, and we flew from Chievres Air Field.

The last few days we've been getting back some of the pilots in the Group that had been P.W.'s [prisoners of war]. The ones I knew who had been P.W.'s for just a short time, it wasn't too bad for them, but some of the other fellows, the boys that had been there for over 6 months were really in ragged shape. I saw several of them get shot down, and that's the most helpless feeling anyone could ever have. You can't do a thing, just pray and hope for them.

I hope this letter finds you as well as I am. Couldn't be better here unless England was in the U.S.A. Keep your fingers crossed. I may get home; the odds are pretty good. It may be a month or two, but don't worry, whatever happens, I'll be O.K. Closing with all my love,
Cobby

May 28, 1945

Hello Darling,
I guess by now you think I've left England, but you're wrong, sweet. I'm just hoping and praying I'll

be with you on August 21, so I can celebrate the most wonderful addition to my life when we got married.

I've just returned from a week's leave in London. I had a pretty good time, spent a lot of money and saw quite a few plays. I ran in to a bunch of my old buddies, and of course a celebration was in order, and celebrating we did! That's about all there is to do for amusement.

Last night we had a big party here on the base and everyone really got stinkin from drinkin. Otherwise things around here are very dull. It's just like being back in the training command again, with ground school, and we can't even buzz anymore. If you get caught it's a $75 fine and you're apt to be grounded a month or more.

Well, my most darling wife, I guess I'm just about rundown. Remember, I love you more than you'll ever know, and I hope I'll be with you again before very long. I love you, darling, Cobby

P.S. The last letter I got the stamp was on straight and you know I demand that they're turned upside down. Don't let it happen again! OK?

May 30, 1945

My Darling Evelyn,

We haven't been doing much of anything, except that the chicken (you know what) is deeper'n hell around here. You can't even spit without going through channels. We've been flying formation, navigation, ground gunnery, aerial gunnery, most anything you can think of, we've been doing. They even have us in ground school everyday, but that isn't so bad because everyone goes, from Colonel down.

The rumors around here are still the same—one day we're flying home for sure, the next day we're on our way to the Pacific. I've quit worrying about it. Darling, I've

*been thinking about our postwar future considerably
the past few days. How would you like to go to college??
We'll have enough money saved up by then and besides,
the Govt. will pay everything for me and pay me $75 a
month. All we'll have to pay for is your tuition and our
board. What do you think? I'm enthusiastic over it now,
but when I get home things may change. Closing now,
dearest, and remember . . . I'll love you always, Cobby*
    P.S. X X X X X X X (Pant! Pant!)

June 3, 1945

My Darling Evelyn,
    *Being today is my day of rest, I decided I'd better
write my honey before she divorces me! I've been doing
a lot of flying these last few days, averaging about three
hours a day. We've been flying cross country mostly
but the other day we flew over to Ireland. Luckily, the
weather was good, and I didn't get lost.*
    *Honey, I hate to bring up this painful subject, but
it seems there is no way around it. Well, you know
this is the first of the month, and we had the regular
crap game, but this time I wasn't so lucky. I need
$200 to clear up my debts. Will you please send me a
money order??? Thank you, sweetheart. I knew you'd
understand. I hate like hell to write you for money. I
could say I won't gamble, but I know I'd be lying. So I
won't say it. I'll exercise better judgment in the future.*
    *Evelyn, I sure was shocked to hear that Ned got it.
But that's the way it goes. You get kind of impersonal
to death after you see a few of your buddies go down.
About a fourth of the guys from Perry are dead now.
Tough, but you gotta go sometime.*
    *Remember, love of my life, I love you more and
more each day and I'll need you forever. Always yours,
Cobby*

June 8, 1945

Dearest Family,

I've been holding off on writing this letter until
I found out definitely when we are going to leave for
the U.S. Rumors are flying fast and furious, and none
are authentic. The latest rumor we're sweating out is
the one that assigns us to the Occupational Air Force.
That is a very disheartening rumor and we're all trying
to discredit it as soon as possible. But according to
all logical arguments (put up by the latrine-o-gram
editors) we will surely be back in the states this
summer. Things around here are dull and unexciting.
We even have two hours of ground school everyday
that includes aircraft recognition (Jap) and all kinds of
repulsive subjects.

Have you heard about the new atomic bomb?
What an awesome weapon. That's the latest topic for
all bull sessions now. With that, I don't see how those
Japs can hold out another 6 months. Pretty optimistic
but that bomb deems it possible in no uncertain terms,
amen.

Yesterday we had a big air show. We flew over
Paris at about 1,000 feet. There were four other
groups besides us which made a total of 180 P-51's,
not counting B-17's from the Eighth Air Force, and
Fighters and Mediums from the 9th AF. The ol' Eiffel
Tower sticks right up there, and some lucky boys from
the 20th Group were down bussing the tower, doing
rolls and in luftberries around it. I guess it was really
an impressive sight from the ground but 3 ½ hours
flying close formation is for the birds, not me. That
was the most exhausting mission I've ever flown.
Combat included.

I haven't received any boxes but the one you all
sent with all the cigs in it. I never did get the pipes
or the toothpaste. Somebody probably hijacked it

and sold the contents to the black market. I did get the 1st Lt. bar you sent me in your letter, Mom. It's really spiffy, in fact, I have it on now. But the critical shortage period is over now, 'cause I got three sets from a friend of mine who made Capt the other day.

The way you folks have talked about the car, I'm kinda anxious to see it. I'll bet it looks really sharp. Pop, now you gotta excuse Mom about not knowing how the car looks, but if it only runs. You know these women don't quite have what it takes to have an interest in something pertaining to mechanical beauty. You know that's about the biggest fault of the breed. But they're kinda nice to have around, especially those two gals of mine, Fritzi and Evy. Yessiree, I wish I had one of em on each arm right now. I believe I'd just love those two gals to death, I do de-clare. That reminds me, Fritzi, you know Evelyn can't cook worth a dern, so I want you to take her aside and give her a few pointers. But don't tell her I told you to.

Well, I guess I'd better be off now. It's way past my bedtime, almost 1 a.m. I'm sure looking forward to those pickled peaches. Yeah man! Hope I don't have to stay here until November. Keep your fingers crossed. All my love, Cobby

June 13, 1945

Hello My Darling,

Today we had a big ceremony of presentation of medals. About fifty guys were decorated but I wasn't one of them. The decorations were mostly Distinguished Flying Crosses, although there were a few Purple Hearts and Silver Stars, and a couple of the paddlefeet got the bronze star for meritorious achievement. General Anderson was down here today to make the awards, and he gave us a little talk. He said we were going to be redeployed to the Pacific through the states, and he

said "while we're in the states we'll get more training."
He also said that while we're here we've really gotta be
on the ball, with no accidents or violations of flying
regulations. And if anything did happen (accident or
violations) the pilot would be court-martialed and
re-evaluated, which means a reduction in grade and
taking away your wings. We've had one fellow in our
squadron already have an accident, a pretty bad one,
too. He washed out a ship in landing. Didn't scratch
him, but the accident board ruled that the pilot was
100% of the cause, and he's sweating out the opinion. He
was the first to foul up under this new policy, and I'm
afraid that they will make an example of him.

Darling, I got the three Cokes you sent today. We
have them out where everyone can see them. I've made
a resolution that I'm not going to drink them until I get
some American whiskey to go with them. Well, darlin', I
guess this winds up my lil' bull session for tonight. Know
what, Mis' Evaline, I sho' do love you, more than you'll
ever know. Remember—I'll love you forever, Cobby

June 15, 1945

My dearest Fritzi and Pop,
    I was real surprised to read in the paper that
Cobby had an oak leaf cluster! It came out in our
paper, too. I'm real proud of that boy! Doesn't it
seem like years since we last saw him?
    Pop, I hope your garden is doing okay.
Mother's going up to Kentucky next month to do
a lot of canning. She's already canned a gang of
cherries. She said she was gonna can everything
she could find, 'cause food is gonna be pretty scarce
next winter.
    I've started filling my cedar chest now, and it's
so much fun! Do I ever have some pretty things for
our home that we'll have someday.

Well, I must close for this time, and you all hug each other tight for me. Lots of love, Evelyn

June 15, 1945

Hello Dearest,
 How's my baby tonight?? In the pink, I hope. I'm fine, only lonely.
 Honey, tell me about this sea going bell hop, Billy Whatsisname that has been sweating out the war on the seat of his britches—they spend so damn much time training those jokers and still they can't fly worth a diddly damn. You know how I feel about those Navy pilots. I don't give 'em a bit of credit. Here the A.A.F. practically single handedly (well almost) wiped out Nazism in Europe, and now we all gotta go over to the Pacific and pull the Navy outa their slump and clean up the job they botched. That Navy pilot with the pretty red car probably has more "bar" time in the U.S.A. than I have flying time. Not that I'm bitching, I'm just envious.
 They say they have so many pilots in the states that they don't know what to do with them. We may have a good chance of staying in the states as a reserve air force and let all those junior birdmen and U.S.O. commandos have a chance to become a hero.
 I'm glad you finally got the Air Medal. I've been sweating that out for quite a while. If that hadn't gotten home, what would I have shown "junior" to prove that his old man was a hero.
 Well, the chickens _ _ _ over here is hip deep to a tall Indian. Believe me, you gotta get a clearance to go to the "brush your teeth" place. Gotta go now—don't forget to send me the dough, please.
 Have I told you I'm just about dying to have you in my arms again? Evelyn, love, I'm yours forever, Cobby

June 20, 1945

My Darling Evelyn,

    I got your letter today, the one in reply to the one I wrote asking you to send me a couple hundred bucks to clear up my gambling debts. I've been sweating it out for quite a few days now. I feel lots better since I found out that you weren't going to divorce me or anything like that. Darling, I know you're right in what you say about gambling, but please listen to my reasons, or excuses if you wish to call them that. To begin with, over here there's only a few things to do—drink, gamble and go out with lewd women. I'll admit to the first two, but plead NOT GUILTY to the latter. And besides, according to my calculations, I've sent home over $500 that I've won since I've been over here. So the $200 the boys won back is to be expected. But all in all, Evelyn, you're absolutely right and I'll heed your advice. No more gambling. Honest.

    Honey, don't you call off your trip to Birmingham on account of that money. Go right ahead and enjoy yourself. Money isn't that important.

    So your sailor friend told you about the "Piccadilly Commando's," huh? Those gals are a disgrace to the female sex. Honestly, it's unbelievable. The way they act. When the black-out was in effect, they used to stand around with flashlights and shine them at you, then on their faces, and say, "five pounds all night, two pounds for a quickie." I guess Piccadilly Circus is the only place in the world where women proposition you right in broad daylight. Except maybe Brussels, only they aren't so persistent. Wait till I get home—some of the things I've seen you'll never believe.

    Hey, did I tell you that they've taken about half of our planes away from us? I still have "ours" tho, baby, and I'm hoping they'll let me keep it till I leave. It sure is a honey, just like you are.

The ground school we have every day is getting to be a pain in the neck. Why, starting next week we have to start taking code. I'm telling you I'm about nuts waiting around here to go home. My nerves are about shot, and it's going to take lots of loving to get me back up to par. It seems as though everyone back home is down on me for not writing, Dad especially. Dammit, I get so low sometimes I feel like a good cry, but instead I go out and get drunk. Gotta go now. Remember, I'll love you forever, Cobby

June 21, 1945

Dearest Evelyn,

This is the second time I've tried to write this letter tonight. I got your 202nd letter today and I was surprised and hurt when I read it. Whether it's my imagination or not, I don't know. But will you please tell me what the hell you meant by asking me if your letters bored me, and if I thought you shouldn't write so often. You know God damn good and well that your letters are all that I live for. I know I'm not worth much, I drink and gamble. I don't write you as much as I should. But by God, I love you, you're my life. If you don't wanta write to me, well don't. I can't make you. But don't you ever ask me again if your letters bore me.

I got the money order you sent today. Thank you, sweet, but I still need another hundred, if you please. You have my word that I won't gamble anymore, due to the very severe lecture I got from you in your letter yesterday. Well darling, keep on loving me and be a good girl. My thoughts are always with you and remember, Evelyn, no matter what happens I'll love you with all my heart. Cobby

P.S. Don't worry about those Piccadilly commandos—I could never be unfaithful to you, sweetheart.

June 24, 1945

Dearest Family,

Well, only one more week in June and then only July and August to sweat out before going home. Boy, I sure will be glad to get out of this country. You spoke of the Gazette carrying an announcement of an oak leaf cluster for my air medal. Well, for your information, I have three clusters now for aerial assaults over enemy territory.

Oh yeah, before I forget it, I got promoted to 1st Lt. yesterday. About time, too. I've been sweating it out for a couple of months and was beginning to think I was going to go home a 2nd. I believe if I had finished my tour and were home now, I could get a discharge. We heard from one of the boys who went home about three months ago, got out on points, and he's now connected with Pan American.

I want to take this opportunity to make a couple of apologies. I want to apologize to you, Mom, for not writing to you on Mother's Day and to you, Dad, for not writing on Father's Day. To be honest I forgot the dates. In fact, I have had quite a few things on my mind for the last month or so. I start worrying about going home, flying or money or anything and wind up thinking of Evelyn.

I hope this letter finds all of you as well as I am. We're kept pretty busy flying, going to ground school, and it takes quite a bit of restraint to keep from going stir crazy.

Clate, I hope to get home in time to see you star in a couple of good football games. All my love, Cobby

June 29, 1945

Dearest Family,
   Well, I can finally give you the lowdown on our movement home. Our primary orders have come in and we're to be ready to leave the 25th of August. So that means I'll probably be home between the tenth and fifteenth of September. I've written Evelyn to meet me in W.Va. We're planning on going on that honeymoon just as soon as I get home. Well, a couple of days after maybe. Glad to hear you're getting the ol' gas buggy into shape, Pop. I haven't driven a car since I was on my last leave before coming over here. I'd like to buy a car of my own if I think I will be stationed in the States for any length of time.
   Hey, Pop, our 1st anniversary is coming up the twenty-first of August and I was wondering if you would send a couple of dozen roses to her for me with this message, "'May each year be better than the last.' All my love, all my life, Cobby." I'll reimburse you when I get home. Thanks a lot.
   I flew on a nice cross country today—flew all over England and part of Scotland. Didn't see much, though. We were flying at 10,000 feet but it sure was a pleasure to fly in nice weather. I'll be seeing you all. Won't be long now. All my love, Cobby

July 1, 1945

My Darling,
   Another month gone by and it won't be long now. Boy, I'm just about going nuts around this place. I've read everything around here between two covers. Good literature, bad literature, sexy literature, all kinds and I am still hunting reading material. I'm about to start on "Strange Fruit" [controversial novel published in 1944, taken from a Billie Holiday song about

*a lynching—horrified critics, was banned in some cities
and seized by the postal service, but became the year's No.
1 fiction best-seller].*

*Tomorrow we're going to start flying some of our
planes to Kassel, Germany for the Occupational Air
Force. We're going to ferry out thirteen of our planes
in the next couple of days, but "ours" is still going to
be in our squadron. It should prove a quite interesting
experience. Then we'll only have twelve more and I
heard we're losing those this month.*

*Gotta go now, darling. Remember I'll Be Yours
Forever, Cobby*

July 1, 1945

Dearest Family,

Here it is the first of July already, and I'm still over
here in Limey land. If the war was still on over here,
I would have almost finished a tour by this time. But
don't get me wrong, I'm not griping because the war is
over, but because I'm not home.

Heard a nasty ol' rumor today. It seems as though
they (the brass) are sending all our planes to Germany
for the Occupational Air Force. I'm flying one to
Kassel tomorrow for the day and coming back by
A.T.C. But can't ever tell about ol' man weather tho,
and we're liable to get socked in for several days. Don't
mind tho. Kinda like to get a look at some of those
krauts.

I was very very shocked to hear that DeWitt
Specht was killed in the Pacific. Why, I can remember
when he was just a little shaver. I don't know why the
Marines take kids that are only seventeen. Pop, you
gotta promise me that you won't give Clate permission
to join up when he's seventeen. I wouldn't be surprised
if the war in Japan lasted a couple of more years. So if

Clate has to go, he'll have to be drafted. Don't let him go until he has to.

Hope you don't have to keep working first trick, Pop, 'cause when I get home I'm kinda hankering to some early morning golf while the dew is still on the ground and the mist hasn't lifted from the hollows. I hear from my lil' honey almost every day. She sure bolsters my morale! You know I didn't believe that I could love a person as much as I love her. Soon as I get home, she and I are going to take off for someplace for about a week, just the two of us on that long awaited honeymoon. I'm really an old married man now, almost a year—10 months, 9 days, 20 hours, and six minutes to be exact. I love her ten times more now than I did when we were married, if that's possible.

Well, I must go now, the sack calls and I gotta get up early for my flight over to kraut land. All my love, Cobby

July 7, 1945

Dearest Family,

Well, another dull week in England has passed by. Only a few more and then the States. Let me tell you about our squadron softball team. We've beat every other team in the group. I'm on first and my hitting is fair. In fact, the hitting of our team is its weakest point. We have a superb pitcher and an exceptional infield. The Col. either catches or plays 2nd base, and he's pretty good. But he loses his temper every now and then and pulls his rank and throws the umpire outa the game. It's really funny sometimes.

All of the Eighth Air Force left in England are the fighter groups, and about six of those have moved to Germany to be in the occupational Air Force. The Bomber jockeys have all flown home. I haven't seen a B-17 or B-24 in the air the last two weeks. I took some pictures of "My Evaline" today. I sure hope that they turn out good 'cause I don't think that she'll be around here much longer. I wouldn't be surprised if all the rest of the airplanes in our group were ferried outa here before the end of the month.

Our food supply has been slashed about 20% and I'm just about to starve. How's about sending me sumpin' to eat, like a potted ham, cheese and crackers and olives and stuff like that?

I'm sure glad you all think so much of Evelyn, I kinda love her myself. I'll sure be glad when this war is over so we can start making you all grandparents. Well, I gotta go now. I sure hope to be seeing you all soon. All my love, Cobby

July 15, 1945

Hello Darling,

I have your picture here before me and every time I look at you my ol' ticker goes bumpty, bumpty, bump in double time. Boy, when your picture does that, I wonder what will happen when I see you in the flesh. It will probably jump right outta me! I sure wish I was with you now. I realize how I love you more and more each day. I often wonder what would have happened to me if I hadn't met you, sweetheart. Remember the first date we had? Wilcox and I met you and Jackie at the U.S.O. and then went to the Commodore Room. And that night in the taxi when I kissed you. I can remember those dates of ours like it was yesterday. And the night in the park—remember, that was the night I found out that I loved you as completely as a man can love a woman. I realize now that I didn't begin to live until I met you. Golly, Evelyn, I have such wonderful memories. They are my most cherished possessions and the wonderful part is that I'll have them always. Yours forever, Cobby

July 15, 1945

Dearest Family,

Another dull week has passed, and that means one less week to sweat out before going home.

Say Mom, the last letter I got from you was right funny. The address was perfect in every way, except that my name wasn't on it. In case you've forgotten, it's 1st Lt. D.A. Webb Jr. 0-2015338! What's the matter, Fritzi, sumpin' on your mind? You don't have a new feller to take my place, have you? Ya better not get someone else to hold your hand when you walk down the street!

Well, master Clate, I hear you're getting a lot of good instruction in kicking and passing the old feetsball. Good show! Don't forget what I told you about playing the game for all you're worth. If you give all you got for 60 minutes a game, you'll rise from mediocre to good, and from good to great.

Don't you worry about me losing that happy go lucky attitude. As much as I like life, I'm afraid that h.g.l. [happy go lucky] attitude is gonna cause me a little grief one of these days. Why right now, some of my buddies are calling me flaky (for flak happy), so you see I'm still daffy. I only have spells of depression because I'm so homesick for you all and Evelyn.

I saw some of the fellows from Salze's group today, and they said that he was grounded for two weeks again, his fourth time, for doing a slow roll on take off. If he gets back to the states alive, I'll be surprised. I haven't been doing much flying lately. The weather isn't quite up to snuff, and besides we only have 10 airplanes in our squadron now. I told you about moving half of our ships (12) to Germany, didn't I?

Sure glad all of the German P.O.W.'s are home. I'll bet they're glad to get out of those hell holes. I sure am thankful that I was lucky. Mom, I kinda feel the same

as you do about Arthur Edwards. I don't think he's
dead either, but he sure has been missing a long time.

Well, I must be going now, gotta write my honey
before I jump in the sack. All my love, Cobby

July 29, 1945

My dearest Pop, Fritzi and Clate,
*I received two letters from Cobby & he doesn't
think he'll be back before September. I've had my
heart set on him coming back next month, but
gosh, I'm thankful he's coming home, so I won't
complain.*

*Last night we went to an Air Show out at Berry
Field. The main part of the show, as far as I was
concerned, were those beautiful P-51's. They flew
all over that field at a terrific speed & every time
they'd pass over, I'd scream that much louder.
Honestly, I've never seen anything go so fast! I
could just picture Cobby in one of them!*

*Wasn't that terrible about that B-25 crashing
into the Empire State Building? That must have
been an awful thing. I'm glad I didn't have to
witness such a tragedy.*

*Well, dearies—guess I'll close for now, so until
next time—All my love, Evaline*

The Plane That Crashed Into the Empire State Building

On the foggy morning of Saturday, July 28, 1945, a U.S. Army B-25
bomber flew through New York City. There was poor visibility, and the
ten-ton, B-25 bomber smashed into the north side of the Empire State

Building. The majority of the plane hit the 79th floor, creating a hole in the building eighteen feet wide and twenty feet high. The plane's high-octane fuel exploded, hurtling flames down the side of the building and inside through hallways and stairwells all the way down to the 75th floor. The plane crash killed 14 people and injured 26 others. Though the integrity of the Empire State Building was not affected, the cost of the damage done by the crash was $1 million.

August 1, 1945

My Darling Evelyn,
    I don't quite know how to start this letter, dear. I daresay it isn't going to be a very good one. I'm pretty bitter today, and disappointed also. I expect that you will feel the same way when I tell you we're not leaving England until November. A notification came in last night that we were transferred to the Strategic Air Reserve, which doesn't call for redeployment to the Pacific. So there's no need to hurry us home. God dammit!!
    Baby, I don't know how I'm going to stand it over here for three more months. Here I was hepped up over getting to be with you again, now this, what a blow! I'm only hoping and praying that the orders will be changed again, and that we come home in September.
    By the time you get this letter, you should have received a V-Mail form telling you not to write me again at this address. Well, disregard that.
    Evelyn remember—whatever happens, no matter how long I'm gone from you, I'll love you deeply and forever, Cobby

August 3, 1945

Hello Darling,
    Here I am again, but I'm still bitter about staying here until November. I'm just hoping that we'll still leave in September. Our C.O., Colonel Mayden, is down at headquarters trying to straighten things out, and everyone is still packing. In fact, everyone around here has an optimistic attitude, so don't give up dearest—I haven't.
    I checked out in the P-47 today. Boy, is that different than a 51, and I don't like it near as well either. But we're all checking out in them because we might have to fly angerbolts (P-47) when we get back to the states.
    I just heard that Col. Mayden has come back from headquarters and said he couldn't find out a thing. I kinda think that "no news" is "good news" and besides our orders to go home on the 25th of this month haven't been canceled yet. Keep your fingers crossed, baby doll.
    Darling, so you get in those loving moods, too. Boy, sometimes when I go to bed, I want you so bad, that I can close my eyes and almost feel you in my arms again. I have a helluva time going to sleep nites when I get in those moods. Yes, dearest, I'm gonna be prepared for all the loving you've got stored up. And I'm gonna take in plenty of dances with you. I wonder how we'll dance together after so long a time. I sure pity your poor feet. Yes, honey, I must admit you do sound a lil' eager, my lil' eager beaver, but I think that I'm just a bit eager myself when it comes to loving you, my sweet. Well, dear, I gotta close now. Keep your fingers crossed, honey. I'll write you as soon as I hear anything definite and remember dear—I love you with all my heart,
Cobby

August 8, 1945

Dearest Family,
  I don't quite know how to tell you all this, but the
facts are, we've had it. I won't be home until November
or later. Our shipment this month has been canceled,
and this group has been assigned to the Strategic
Air Reserve, which means we've lost our priority for
transportation. Now if I don't have to go to the army
of occupation, I'll be home before Christmas, I hope.
Everything is snafued over here. I guess because the
Germans are beaten they're gonna forget all about
us poor fighter pilots and leave us to the mercy of
the bloody limeys. Why, some of the fellows are even
talking about taking out citizenship papers! (bad joke)
  This means that all the plans that you have made
are shot in the rear. So you all had better take your
vacation and leave me out of the plans. Honestly, I've
never been so disappointed in my whole life. I guess
Evelyn will take it pretty hard. Why don't you all insist
that she visit you or go down to see her.
  Now that Russia has declared war on Japan, and
with the new atomic bomb, I expect the war in the
Pacific will be over in a few months. At least I hope
so. Maybe we'll get home at least a few days sooner if
the Japanese war is over by the first of the year. Some
of the fellows claimed to have heard over the radio
today that the Japs were ready to accept the ultimatum
made at the Potsdam Conference, but I listened to the
radio all day and didn't hear a thing. I hope that it's
straight dope and not just another rumor. I think the
Japs should have seen the light by now with the atomic
bomb and Russia's entry into the war. I know damn
good and well that I wouldn't want to be in Japan right
now. I believe that I'd rather be flying combat missions
in the Pacific than be here. The boredom here is awful.
Believe me when I fly it's only going to be four hours a
month, to get my flight pay in and perhaps half of that
will be flown by the pencil.
  Well, I gotta go now. I just wrote to let you know
how I stand over here. I don't think I'll be home for at

least three months. Sorry this had to happen, but you know the Army. What a bunch of Rum Dums [dapper gentlemen who are always tipsy]. **All my love, Cobby**

Potsdam Conference

The Allied Conference of World War II was held at Potsdam, a suburb of Berlin, from July 17 to August 2, 1945, to discuss a peace settlement with Germany and reconstruction, and agreement on the prosecution of Nazi war criminals. The chief participants were U.S. President Harry S. Truman, British Prime Minister Winston Churchill, and Soviet Premier Joseph Stalin. The Potsdam Conference established four occupation zones in Germany to be administered by the Soviet, British, American, and French armies of occupation. An Allied Control Council made up of representatives from the four Allies was to deal with matters affecting Germany as a whole. In addition, the leaders outlined a plan for Japan's unconditional surrender and discussed including the use of the United States' new weapon (the atomic bomb) if Japan did not comply. From the conference, an ultimatum demanding unconditional surrender or face heavier air attacks was made.

August 10, 1945

Hello Sweetheart,
 I've just finished writing the folks and telling them I won't be home for at least another three months. I hate to see Pop's face when he reads that. He'll probably write his congressman and give him a good chewing out. Wish I could give someone a long call on this deal.
 Now I'm sweating out the Army of Occupation. They've already taken 20 of the ground officers from the group, and a hundred or more enlisted men are going in the next couple of days. So you can understand why we're on pins and needles. I don't think there is any need

for pilots over there, at least I hope not. I can't see why they don't get some of the brown-nosing so-and-so's that have been in the states since the war has started and send them over here to see the world. Some of the fellows going to Germany have been over here for over two years. Most of them are drunk tonight and by God, I don't blame them. If I go to the Army of Occupation, I'm gonna get drunk and stay that way for at least a week, so help me.

Darling, my letters for the next few days are gonna be pretty sorry, until I'm reconciled to the fact that I have to stay over here an additional three months. I'm getting bitter all over again just thinking about it. Or maybe it's just sinking in to that thick skull of mine, just how much it means to be here all that time. Listening to me rant and rave will probably make you as P.O.'d as I am, so I better shut my big mouth and go to bed. Keep loving me, Evelyn, and remember, I'll love you always, Cobby

P.S. Honey, what is this stuff about some guys following you in a car after you came home from the circus? You know what I'd have done—I think you should have called the cops. If someone ever pulls that stuff when you're with me . . . well, I hate to think of what I'd do. Baby, you be careful, I don't know what I'd do if anything ever happened to you because you're my life and without you I'd be useless.

August 13, 1945

Hello Darling,
  I'm writing this letter so it will reach you on the twenty-first of this month, or close to that day. In case you have forgotten, dear, the twenty-first of August, nineteen hundred and forty-four was the day I began to live. You made me the happiest guy in the world, Evelyn, when you said yes that night down at the train station. Although we're far apart in miles, I feel we are very close in spirit on this day.
  Remember up in our "Bridal Suite" after we had said our "I do's" and you and I and Jimmy, Butch and Step were sitting around having a glass of beer, how embarrassed we were. I thought they would never leave. And when they finally did leave—I don't know which of us was more scared. I guess we were both pretty nervous. Nevertheless, I'll never forget that night, the night we became man and wife, and all of us belonged to each other.
  Dearest, I'm sorry that I'm not able to send you something to commemorate this most eventful day in our lives, but I can't get a thing over here, not even a card. I wrote Dad and told him to send you some roses for me. I hope you received them, my dearest.
  I'm enclosing in this letter a picture of our plane. It's a pretty good shot, so hang on to it. It's the only one I have and I want to get it enlarged and tinted when I get home.
  Sweetheart, I'm going to close now. I only hope this letter will ease the pain of our being separated on the day which is most dear to my heart. Keep your chin up. I'll be home before you know it. May each year be happier than the last. I'll always love and cherish you, Evelyn. All my love forever, Cobby

August 14, 1945

Dearest Family,
I guess you all have been sticking pretty close to the radio just like we have. I guess by the time you get this letter, the war will be over, or Japan will be utterly devastated by the atomic bombs. The latest opinion over here is that the Japs are stalling for time and all of us are in favor of blowing those treacherous Japs right off the face of the earth. I guess if the war is over in the next few days, we ought to have a pretty good chance of leaving here for the states before November.
I guess Evelyn is pretty disappointed, but little I can do. With things as they are, I don't know when I'll be home. I'll believe I'm on the way home when I get on the boat. Well, gotta go now. Your devoted son,
Cobby

JAPAN SURRENDERS

By July 1945, Allied bombs had destroyed half of Tokyo and many other towns and cities. The Allies thought that a complete invasion of Japan was necessary to end the war, but that one million soldiers could die in the invasion. Japan was willing to negotiate a peace, but had indicated an unwillingness to accept unconditional surrender and a just peace. An ultimatum from the Potsdam Conference several weeks earlier had been issued and ignored. On August 6, 1945, the United States dropped the first atomic bomb on Hiroshima, Japan. Over 92,000 Japanese were killed. President Truman then called on the Japanese government to surrender. The Japanese did not respond, and the United States dropped an even larger bomb over the city of Nagasaki on August 9, 1945. Over 40,000 additional Japanese people were killed. On August 15, 1945, Emperor Hirohito announced that the nation was surrendering. On September 2, 1945, on the deck of the battleship USS *Missouri*, the surrender documents were signed and the war in the Pacific was over.

The New York Times

August 14, 1945

JAPAN SURRENDERS,
END OF WAR!

EMPEROR ACCEPTS ALLIED
RULE; MacARTHUR SUPREME
COMMANDER
Washington, August 14. Japan
today unconditionally surrendered
the hemispheric empire taken by
force and held almost intact for more
than two years against the rising
power of the United States and its
Allies in the Pacific war. The bloody
dream of the Japanese military caste
vanished in the text of a note to the
Four Powers accepting the terms of
the Potsdam Declaration of July 26,
1945.[52]

END OF WORLD WAR II

The wars against Germany, Italy, and Japan were finally over after five long years of misery, pain, suffering, courage, and endurance of people in many countries across the globe. World War II killed more people, cost more money, damaged and destroyed more property, affected the lives of more people, and caused more far-reaching political and economic changes than any other war in history. Official casualty sources estimate battle deaths at nearly 15 million military personnel and civilian deaths at over 38 million. It is very difficult to calculate civilian deaths from land battles, aerial bombardment, political and racial executions, disease and famine and other war related causes. In addition, there were over 21 million refugees, many displaced from their homes, cities, and countries. In the United States, sixteen million American men and women served in uniform during World War II and more than 400,000 were killed. Hundreds of thousands of other soldiers came home from the war wounded and/or with permanent physical and mental disabilities. Every community across the country mourned the loss of a family member or friend who died or suffered permanent mental and/or physical disabilities in this war. People in America and in many other countries around the world joined together in celebration and thankfulness that the ongoing nightmare and horror of war had ended. Recovery would be a long process.

One branch of the military, United States Army Air Forces, reported that 88,119 airmen died in service. The total aircraft losses by the USAAF from December 1941 to August 1945 were 65,164 planes, with 43,581 lost overseas and 21,583 within the Continental United States, during training.

August 16, 1945

My Darling,
Well, it's finally all over now. We really had quite a party over here V-J night. I was in bed listening to the news (it was after midnight) on the radio when they announced that the Japs had accepted the surrender terms. We all got up and went over to the bar. All the officers on the field were there and the drinks were on the house. What a brawl. The scotch and bourbon flowed like water and I was there lapping up my share. I finally got back to the sack around dawn and slept all day. From all I gather by the newspapers, and the radio, I guess the States really went wild. I sure wish I could have been there with you celebrating. I guess you really raised cain.
We are all anxiously awaiting some word of what we're going to do. Everybody seems to think that the end of the wars will make a big difference when we'll be going back to the states. As I've told you before, this group is a high point outfit, with more men eligible for discharge than almost any other group in the E.T.O. Whether that will make any difference in the shipping orders I don't know—I can only hope!
I'm pretty hepped up these days about us going to school when the war's over, I mean when I get discharged. I don't want to go unless you want to go

with me. It oughta be fun, don't ya think? Well, we'll talk
that over when I get home, honey.

Well, in nine more days you'll have been Mrs. Webb
for a whole year, and nine months of that—a war
widow. Well, when I get home I will sure make up for
lost time. I can almost taste the sweetness of your kisses
now, sweetheart. Gonna close now, sweet, keep writing
me, and give all my love to mama and pappy. I'll love
you forever, Cobby

August 17, 1945

Hello Dearest,
Well, V-J day plus three has drawn to a dreary close.
The ceiling has been zero for the last week. Even the
birds are walking. But even if the weather does clear up,
we won't be able to fly, because all of the ships in the 3rd
Air division have been grounded. We were transferred
to the 3rd from the 1st just a few days ago. Why—none
of us can guess.

I got a letter from you today, telling me you
expected the folks the next day. I don't know why I'm
always kept in the dark in this family. I didn't know a
thing about them going way down in the Deep South.
By damn, I'm going to be kept informed around here or
by golly, there's going to be some changes made in the
personnel of the Webb clan.

I didn't plan to write you tonight, darling, but I'm
so blue and downhearted I couldn't help but write you
for consolation. All of us are singing the blues because
we're not going home as scheduled. I don't know why
they are keeping us over here now that the war's over. I
for one am ready to be indoctrinated on how to become
a civilian. If only I had you to love and comfort me, I'd
be happy sitting on top of the North Pole.

Just think, Evelyn, in three more days you will have
been Mrs. Webb for a whole year. I never will forget

those first three months of bliss. The rest of our lives will be spent reliving those wonderful days. The only thing is that I'm a little impatient in getting started. I lie awake at night thinking of what I'm going to say when I hold you in my arms again. I get cold shivers just thinking about it. I was just thinking about the first time I ever kissed you. In the cab, remember? We were taking you & Jackie home and I remember asking the cab driver to wait a few minutes. You looked at me kinda funny and said quite dryly, "There will be no need of waiting, we're going right in." Needless to say, I felt taken down a few pegs. In fact my ego hit an all time low that night and I spent some time recovering.

And remember how you used to sing "The Right Kind of Love?" I still know the words and I don't believe I'll ever forget them. I better sign off now before I gush right off the page. Remember what I've always said—I'll love you always, Cobby

August 20, 1945

Still England

Dearest Family,
Another week has slowly gone by and still no hope of leaving here in the near future. Our service group is supposed to leave sometime this week, but the fighter group is still going to be in England no one knows how long. Today I flew. Yep the weather was flyable for the first time in two weeks. I was so happy to get in the wild blue yonder that I let my enthusiasm get away with me and got myself grounded for making "too hot a take-off." Whoa! Wait up and I'll tell what happened. I took off on a routine flight and held her on the deck until I hit around 200 mph, almost running down a couple of limey's (small loss) and then I racked it up in a big ol' chandelle. That's all I did, and the squadron

officer got P.O.'d 'cause he thought that was too hot, but I think he's going to relent, and put me back on flying duty. Oh well, live and learn. The weather probably won't be good enough for flying again for two weeks, so why worry.

I got the first letter Evy had written since she found out that I wasn't coming home until November. Needless to say, she's disappointed beyond words. I hated to write her and tell her such depressing news. But she, like the great gal she is, took it smiling. I guess I'm just about the luckiest guy in the world, besides you, Pop.

Hey, I believe this is the first letter I've written you all since V-J day. I guess you all are as happy over there as we are over here. What a celebration here at ol' Bodney. Everyone went nuts and all ships were grounded so no one would take the roof off the place. No more dodging bullets, hooray! I was kinda sweating out the Pacific. I haven't been off the base since V-J day, but the reports the fellows bring back, from Liberty Runs, wow!! Dancing in the streets and a kind word from the Limeys to the Yanks for a change. They're still celebrating in the towns here. It's customary to celebrate for a week, when such a big thing happens. It was the same on V-E day—really a celebration. The declaration of peace should make our chances to return home a little better. Good night. All my love, Cobby

P.S. I got a notice from Miami today, asking whether or not I intended to go back to school. I said yes. Also read a notification of Jim Bussards's death at Okinawa in June. You remember Bussie, a little guy and halfback on Miami's team—really swell. He was one of my best friends when I was there and his death was a shock.

August 21, 1945

Hello Darling,
Happy anniversary, sweetheart. I've been thinking
about you all day, dearest. I spent what little money
I had left over at the bar celebrating. I only wish I
could have been with you on this momentous occasion.
Although we're far apart in miles, I felt that we were
close in spirit on this day. I hope you will be in my
arms, where you belong, before too long. Well darling,
I'd better close now. I hope you are as glad that we're
married as I am. I'll always love and cherish you,
Evelyn. All my love forever, Cobby

August 21, 1945

Dearest Family,
I'm a little off my letter schedule this week,
holding out until I heard some news. All of the
enlisted men in the group with 85 points or more left
here for the states yesterday. We lost 3/4 of the enlisted
men in our squadron, and the other two squadrons
have lost as many. But we haven't heard a thing about
what is going to happen to the pilots. We should hear
something soon.
We only have 4 planes to fly now, as there are only
enough A.M.'s to maintain four. Of course, mine is one
of them. By golly, "My Evaline" is the best damn ship
in the E.T.O.
I'm sure glad you had such a swell time down in
Tennessee, and I'm not surprised that you like Mamma
and Pappy Lassiter. They are the most gracious and
hospitable people I've ever known. Oh yes, Pop, thank
you ever so much for ordering those roses for my baby.
I haven't heard from her yet, but I know she will be
thrilled!

In your last letter you averaged 36 mph on your return from Nashville and asked how we fliers would acclimatize ourselves to ground speeds after flying. Well, I, for one, am not planning to return to ground speeds, not wholly anyway. I'm planning on buying an army surplus plane. Laugh, go on, laugh, I know what you are thinking. I'm full of wild ideas but I plan to get one for less than a thousand bucks. And as soon as I get home and get discharged, I'm going to get myself a commercial license and see what post war aviation holds for me. After all, flying is the only thing I know. And I don't think I can afford to let all my training go to waste.

Clate, I have a Nazi knife for you, and it has quite a history. It was used to kill a member of the French resistance fighters by a kraut soldier, and the friends of the fellow killed, used it to slay the jerry soldier. I've cleaned it up, but when I got it, you could still see traces of blood.

Sure was too bad that Bill got killed, but flak isn't particular. Well, I guess I'd better sign off for now. All my love, Cobby

The Adjusted Service Rating, or "Point System" as described by Cobby, was developed as a measurement tool to determine when a soldier could be discharged or sent home following the war, as hundreds of thousands of soldiers had to be discharged home and/or deployed to other bases and/or armies of occupation. Each soldier was awarded a number of points for his participation in the military that included total months of service in the military, each month in service stationed overseas, any combat awards received, and the number of children he had at home in the states. The higher the score, the higher the probability to be sent home for discharge.

August 21, 1945

My dearest Fritzi, Pop, & Clate,
I'm so thrilled I just don't know what to say!
My flowers from Cobby came today & they are
the most beautiful roses I've ever laid my eyes on.
I was so shocked when they were delivered that I
couldn't say anything. I also received a letter from
Cobby today & it was the sweetest thing. So sweet,
in fact, that I nearly cried. Honestly—I know I
have the sweetest husband in the world. This has
been one of the happiest days in my life. I just
needed Cobby here to make it perfect!
Well—you all excuse my short note, but I just
wanted to let you know that I received flowers and
a letter. Kiss each other for me. Lots of love, Evelyn

August 28, 1945

Hello Darling,
Well, things are beginning to happen around here.
About 250 enlisted men have been alerted to go home
tomorrow. In fact, all the enlisted men who have over
85 points are going. So I guess we'll soon be hearing
something about leaving here, either for the states or for
Germany. I have over enough points to get a discharge,
so I don't think I'll go to the Occupational Air Force. I
have 63 points and under the new plan in the AAD, 1st
LT's with 58 or more points are eligible. So as soon as I
hit the states, I think I'll get a discharge. Hooray! Then
we can live like human beings again!
I'm sure glad, darling, that you received the roses
OK. I was afraid that you wouldn't get them, and you'd
think I'd forgotten that day, over a year now, that you
became Mrs. Webb. I'll never forget, Evelyn. I received
the pictures you all took while the folks were down, and
they made a big ol' lump come up in my throat. They

really made me homesick. If you were only here in my arms, I'd stay in this Godforsaken hole gladly for the rest of my life. I guess you know by now that you're the main spar in my wings of life. I hope you are as glad as I am that we are married.

Did you ever hear about the girl who went to the hospital and asked the nurse on duty to see the upturn. "You mean the intern, don't you?" said the nurse. "Yes, I guess," answered the girl. The nurse asked "why," and the girl answered, "to get a contamination." "You mean examination," said the nurse. The girl said "yes" and "I want to go to the fraternity ward." The nurse asked if she didn't mean the maternity ward. The girl replied, "What the hell! Interns, upturns, contamination, examination, fraternity ward, maternity ward. What's the difference? All I know is that I haven't demonstrated for two months and I think I'm stagnant!" I got a big kick out of that joke.

Oh about those pajamas—you know how I feel about them. I much prefer gowns, or better still, nothing at all. Don't you think we've been married long enough not to be shy? I do. I've just spent about twenty minutes looking for a Stars & Stripes to send you. It has some pictures of French bathing beauties in it, and I wanted you to see how scanty the suits were. The tops only covered the nipples (honest to God) and the tops of the pants were about three inches below the navel. Didn't leave hardly anything to the imagination. Hey! I bet you'd look cute in a suit like that!

Gotta go now, my sweet. Write lots and remember, I'm always faithfully yours, Cobby.

September 17, 1945

Dearest Family,

I guess I'd better come straight to the point, and not beat around the bush any. Yesterday I received orders to go to the Occupational Air Force, in

Germany. I'm leaving tomorrow with 35 other fellows, on B-17's. All pilots with less than 75 points are going to the Occupational Air Force. But in this shipment they first took the fellows with less than 63 points. I had 62 so I was included. Out of England alone there are 500 pilots leaving for Germany tomorrow, so you can imagine how many of us are really being shafted. I've just finished writing Evelyn, and I know she's going to be disappointed as hell, but not anymore than I am. I don't have the slightest idea when I'll get home now. God only knows. I only hope that I can keep from going nuts. I didn't write last week, 'cause I thought some shaggy deal like this was cooking. This is precisely what I've been afraid of. Oh well, somebody has to get the dirty end of the stick.

I'm mailing a box home to you and it contains summer uniforms, flying gloves, also a R.A.F. type oxygen mask. The oxygen mask is a souvenir for you, Clate, and you can have any other stuff you want. Those gloves might come in pretty handy this winter. They sure did the trick at 30,000 ft.

Well, I'm going to close now. I sure hope I get to see you all in the next 5 or 10 years. All my love, Cobby

September 19, 1945

My Darling Evelyn,

I'm still at Bodney. We were supposed to leave here Monday. I've got my orders, cleared the post and now we're just waiting for transportation. On our orders it states that we will go to someplace near Frankfort. There is a rumor out, that a directive has just been received that states if you're assigned to the Occupational Air Force, the MAXIMUM time you'll be over there is six months. If that's true it won't be so bad. I'm looking forward to this occupation like I'd look forward to a prison sentence.

Gotta letter from Dad the other day. You should have heard him rave about Clayton in the first game of the season this year. He said Clate made two of the team's four touchdowns, did all the passing and kicking, and did quite a bit of blocking and tackling on the side. I was counting pretty heavily on getting to see him in action this fall.

I keep looking forward to the day when you're in my arms again, all snuggled up, never to be separated again. I'm forever yours, Cobby

REFERENCES

1   "The Vichy Regime: July 1940-August 1944." The Jewish Virtual Library,
    A Division of the American-Israeli Cooperative Enterprise. Accessed
    September 25, 2012. http://www.jewishvirtuallibrary.org/jsource/
    Holocaust/VichyRegime.html

2   "Holocaust History: Liberation of Nazi Camps." The United States
    Holocaust Memorial Museum Website. Accessed August 15, 2012. http://
    www.ushmm.org/wlc/en/ article.php?ModuleId=10005131

3   "Battle for Germany." The Oxford Companion to American Military
    History Website. Accessed December 8, 2011. http://www.answers.com/
    topic/battle-for-germany

4   "Italian partisans kill Mussolini, 1945." The Official Website of the BBC
    News Network Website. Accessed December 27, 2012. http://news.bbc.
    co.uk/onthisday/hi/ dates/stories/april/28/newsid_3564000/3564529.stm

5   "More information about: Adolf Hitler." The Official BBC News Network
    Website. Accessed December 27, 2012. http://www.bbc.co.uk/history/
    people/adolf_hitler

6   Kennedy, E. The War in Europe is Ended! New York Times on the Web
    Learning Network. May 7, 1945. Retrieved February 28, 2013. http://
    www.nytimes.com/learning/general/ onthisday/big/0507.html

7   Rosenberg, Jennifer. The Plane That Crashed into the Empire State Building.
    20th Century History, at the About.com Website. Retrieved August 30,
    2012. http://history1900s.about.com/od/1 940s/a/empirecrash.htm

8   "Potsdam Conference." The Encyclopædia Britannica Online Website.
    Accessed September 25, 2012 from http://www.britannica.com/EBchecked/
    topic/472799/Potsdam-Conference

9   "Japan signs underconditional surrender." The Official BBC News Network
    Website. Accessed December 27, 2012. http://news.bbc.co.uk/onthisday/
    hi/dates/stories/september/2/newsid_3582000/3582545.stm

10 Krock, A. Japan Surrenders, End of War! New York Times on the Web
    Learning Network, August 14, 1945. Retrieved February 28, 2013. http://
    www.nytimes.com/learning /general/onthisday/big/0814.html

11 "World War II; Forces and resources of the European Combatants,
    1939." Encyclopædia Britannica Online Website. Accessed September
    25, 2012. http://www.britannica.com/EBchecked/topic/648813/
    World-War-II/53533/   Forces-and-resources-of-the-European-
    combatants-1939

12 "Defense Casualty Analysis System: World War II." The Official Website
    of the Department of Defense of the United States of America. Accessed

217

August 11, 2012. https://www.dmdc.osd.mil/dcas/pages/casualties_ww2. Xhtml

13 "USAAF Statistical Summary of World War II." Wikipedia, The Free Encyclopedia. Accessed December 28, 2012. http://en.wikipedia.org/w/ index.php?title=United_States_ Army_Air_Forces&oldid=529469847

CHAPTER TWELVE.

Occupational Air Force in Germany, 1945

In the summer of 1945, Joseph Stalin, Soviet leader; Winston Churchill, British Prime Minister; and Harry Truman, U.S. President, met at the Potsdam Conference to discuss the unconditional surrender of Japan and to negotiate the terms for the end of World War II. A major issue at the time was how to handle Germany. During the interim period, Germany would be divided into four zones to be run by the four occupying powers, including the United States, Britain, France, and the Soviet Union.

Cobby was assigned to 472nd Air Service Group outside of Nuremberg as part of the Army of Occupation from September, 1945 to February, 1946. He was appointed Provost Marshal of the base and commanding officer of the guard section. In this capacity, Cobby was responsible for security, protection of military property, and behavior of troops on the base.

September 23, 1945

My Darling Evelyn,

Well, we're all set to go to Germany tomorrow. This makes the third or fourth time we've been all set to go. I'll sure be glad to get away from here. The sooner I get to Germany, the sooner I get home. I'll bet we'll have so much love stored up that we won't need any heat in the house all winter. I shudder to think what would have happened if you had gotten on that train that night August 20. You know, the thought of you is all that keeps me going sometime. Sometimes I just can't understand how I persuaded you to take the big step with me. Must be hidden talent of which I know nothing. Thank you, Evelyn, for taking a chance on me. I'll always do my best to be a good husband to you.

Yesterday about 25 glider pilots came into the group. They're high point men from the Continent who are taking our place in the group. All of these guys are *loaded down with money they made selling stuff on the black market. They said you can get $200 for a carton of cigarettes and anywhere from $500 to $1000 for a wrist watch. That's a lot of money. Well, Darling, I guess I'll close now and remember, I'll love you forever. Cobby*

October 1, 1945

My Darling Evelyn,
*   I'm in Nuremberg, Germany in a service group, (this will kill ya) and I'm a ground pounder. I don't know what my job will be yet, since this is only my second day here. But I've talked to the C.O. and I think I might be either an M.P. officer or an engineering officer. Whatever it is, it won't be connected with flying, although I will have the opportunity to get in my flying time. Boy, when I found out I was going to be a ground officer, I damn near blew my top! What a blow. But things are looking pretty good. We have good quarters, the food is superb, and there isn't too much work connected with any of the jobs. The drinks here are the equivalent of 10 cents per drink but all they have is cognac and I don't like that worth a damn. The beer is free but it's not very good either.*
*   I've sure seen a lot of Germany in the last few days. You should see what the Air Force did to Nuremberg. There are only two buildings in the whole city. They are the Red Cross Club and the Opera House. Everything else is rubble. There are D.P.'s (displaced persons) doing all the work around here—the housework, laundry, dry cleaning, everything.*
*   Well, my darling wife, I guess I'd better close now. Send me more pictures, please, and write lots. My morale is pretty low these days. Always remember, I'll love you forever, Cobby*

October 4, 1945

Hello Darling,

Boy, have I been busy lately! I have a bunch of jobs now. I'm Provost Marshall, Special Service Officer, Athletic Officer and what have you. And I don't know a diddly damn about any of them. Because I'm the Provost Marshall, all the boys are calling me "sheriff" and my office "the courthouse." I'm kinda glad I'm in the Service Group now. We have a bunch of German cars we drive all the time. Besides that, we have a P-51 and a piggyback P-51 and that's not all. We have a cub, too, all of which can be flown at any time by the ten pilots in the Service Group. We're practically assured of our flying time plus plenty more. All the departments in the service group are very short on men, with guys going home, etc. Well, my M.P. section is down pretty low and last night one of the men who was to go on duty got drunk and refused to go and then he hit the Corporal of the Guard. So this morning I had to chew him out good and turn him over to the C.O. and we're going to court martial him, I think. More damned trouble.

I checked out in the cub the other day and had more fun. That lil cub sure is nothing but a kite with an engine. After I get home, I'm gonna get an airplane, probably a cub. I'll teach you to fly and we'll have a time of our lives flying around the country.

One thing about this place, no one does any work. All the Germans do it! And you should hear me trying to speak to them in French, Spanish, English and everything but German, which I don't comprehend at all. Gotta go, Sweetheart. Remember, hon, I'll love you forever, Cobby

October 5, 1945

Dearest Family,

I suppose you've been wondering what has happened to me since I haven't written in several days. As you know I'm now in the O.A.F. which is in the 9th Air Force, but I'm not assigned to a flying job. I'm the Provost Marshall and Special Service Officer for the 472nd Air Service Group. At first I was a little browned off at having such an assignment (me the hottest pilot in the E.T.O.!) But now I'm beginning to think I have one of the best deals to be had in the OAF. We can fly anytime we want to and we all (10 pilots including me) have German cars at our disposal. It's kind of funny—none of us have ever held jobs of this type before and there is very little work to be done on the base, although there was a little excitement here last night. They caught some German who works on the field here stealing food. He's in a cell right now waiting until the major sees him. I don't have the slightest idea what is going to be done with him.

I'm only about 5 or 10 miles from Nuremberg. The country here is beautiful and pleasant, our barracks are tops and the food is superb. Everything is wonderful, only on the wrong side of the world. I think I may get home by the first of the year if I'm lucky. I'd give my left arm to be home this very minute. I miss Evelyn something fierce. I do declare that lil ol' gal is in for plenty of affection (sounds better than loving). I haven't heard from anyone in a couple of weeks, but I'm sure it is because I've been moving so darn much. Don't worry, I'll be home toot sweet [tout de suite, immediately]. **All my love, Cobby**

October 10, 1945

Hello My Darling,

How is my one and only this fine day? I just received a bunch of letters from you, eight to be exact, and my morale is soaring with leaps and bounds. I'm glad that you took the delay in our plans with such grace. I was afraid that you might do something drastic, like divorce or sumpthin'.

Say, did I ever tell you about the time I got married to the sweetest, most wonderful lil rebel in the whole world? By damn! Remind me to tell you about that sometime. It's really a terrific love story and I love to tell it! It's not so good on paper so I think I'd better keep it to myself until I can have you for a real live audience.

I saw a couple of good games over the week-end between a couple of infantry teams. The games were held at Soldier's Field in Nuremberg, which, when the Nazis had control, was the place that Hitler held all those mass meetings and rallies, which you used to see in the news reels before the war. It was a colossal place. I'm gonna try and take some pictures from the air, and I'll send you some.

Darling, I wish you would go up to W. Va. for a visit. My folks are sadly in need of some cheering up after they found out I won't be home for a while. Besides I want you to see Clate play football, so you can give me all the details. I hear from Dad about his playing, but he's prejudiced, and Mom more than Dad, and Clate's too modest. I know they're wild to see you!!

Boy, have I been busy today. First thing this morning, the boys (MP's) found some gal in a fellow's room shacking up and by one o'clock we had three German whores in the clink. And what beasts they are, my God they look as if they're dosed up with everything under the sun.

Yesterday an ex Luftwaffe pilot came in to see me and asked if the group needed any pilots. You could have knocked me over with a feather I was so flabbergasted! As if the Air Corps didn't have enough "stick & rudder" boys.

I haven't been flying much lately, and the little flying I do is in a cub (L-4). When I first flew it, I kinda thought that it was fun. But any more I get just a trifle bored going along up there at 65 or 70 mph. Oh those Peter five ones, how I love 'em! But the weather here is about 100% better than that in England and the countryside is beautiful.

Did you hear the joke about the guy who claimed he could live on love? Well, it seemed this couple got married and instead of eating at mealtimes, they went to bed (not to sleep either). This kept on for a while. One night the old man came home from work and found his wife sliding down the banisters on the stairs. So he asked her, "What do you mean by sliding down the banister like that, darling?" She looked at him coyly and said "Why, honey, I'm warming up supper!" I love you more than anything on God's green earth. All my love forever, Cobby

"The Sheriff of R-29" [Cobby Webb]

"Me and puddlejumper" [Cobby Webb]

October 20, 1945

Hello Darling,

I haven't been as busy these last couple of days since I've been in the Army. Boy, these Krauts sure are a headache. Yesterday, we caught an ex SS Trooper working here on the base. He had false discharge papers, so they took him to the Military Govt. Office in Nuremberg for questioning. Did I tell you what happened to the kraut we caught stealing food? He got 9 months and another got 6 months for stealing a gallon of gasoline. Boy! They don't monkey around with those babies around here.

Say, honey bun, did I ever tell you how much I love you? I'm constantly thinking of you and how you used to kiss me and make love to me. You know, Evelyn, I want you so bad that I hurt inside. Sometimes I wake up at night, absolutely sure that you're there with me, and when I find out that I've been dreaming, I feel like beating my head against the wall.

So you're cold! So am I. Just you wait until I get home. We'll stay broke all the time, buying beds. We'll probably burn'em right to the floor and melt all the snow for miles around. Why, if the city of New York would install us a bed on the ground floor of the Empire State Building, they wouldn't have to buy coal all winter! What do you think about that? I know, I know, don't tell me. I must be getting crude in my old age, or maybe it's just because I haven't held you in my arms for so long.

Charlie Provost just came in and told me that someone had taken one of the medic's ambulances last night and had abandoned it. Either the driver left it of his own free will or someone jumped him. More damned trouble around here, but leave it to Sheriff Webb—he'll catch the culprit or culprits.

Well, sweetie pie, I guess I better close now. Be sure to give my love to Mama & Pappy and remember dearest, I'll love you forever, Cobby

October 25, 1945

Hello Darling,

I just received four letters from you and I'm just as happy as can be. You'd be surprised how much a letter from you lifts my morale.

Say my lil' sweet patootie, on this furniture deal, what ya say we let it ride for a while, huh? 'Cause when I get home I wanta try and go to school for a while, and we don't wanta be bothered with furniture, and we don't even have a place to put it. Let's get a house first and then furnishings to suit the house, not a house to suit the furnishings. Now don't you agree? We'll plan all of this out when I get home. Sweetheart, you know planning a home is the most important part, and more fun besides. You know what I'd like? I'd like to build our own place just the way we want it. But that dream is quite some distance away. Besides, in a few months I'll be joining the long file of unemployed. When I get home and get discharged, I'm going to take a couple of months vacation and concentrate on rehabilitating myself to civilian life again and deciding what I'm going to do. I'm trying to save enough out of my pay to have enough for some Civies and last us long enough to decide what we're going to do. If I can do that, we won't have to touch the money we've saved.

Baby doll, your description of Jackson's wedding was just a lil' incoherent. I guess you were a bit excited. What I want to know is, did you kiss the bridegroom? I guess once was OK, but with all of these weddings you are planning, I'm afraid kissing the bridegroom is going to become a habit. Now honey, you don't want to be the cause of wrecking a woman's married life before it even gets started would you? That's just what's going to happen when you go around kissing bridegrooms—I know how you kiss. Yep, your kisses are like a glimpse into heaven!

Been having a lil' trouble today. Got another G.I. in the guard house. He was A.W.O.L. for a month, so he got one year confinement and a dishonorable discharge. But his case is being reviewed and I believe that the D.D. will be refuted. Honey, you and I have the same views on these Kraut women. I can't understand how these guys have forgotten the war so quickly. By golly, if I had my way, there wouldn't be any fraternizing, and I would turn them over to the Russians. You know the Germans are really scared of the Russians.

Say my lil' sweet patootie, what's this deal on the Navy? Since when did those sea goin' bell-hops take over Nashville? What did they do, sail up the Cumberland River?

Gosh hon, I'm sorry that you're not going to be able to go to W.Va. for a visit. Mom and Dad are going to be terribly disappointed. I think they love you more than they do me. They've always wanted a daughter. I've been writing Pop about how I hope you have learned to cook and Pop said you couldn't miss because your mom is such a good cook. But for me, seeing is believing! But you shouldn't worry, baby, I won't be hard to please after eating army chow. Hell! Once I get you in my arms I'm not going to worry about such a trivial thing as food. I can almost feel your arms around me now and taste the sweetness of your lips. I'll love you forever, Cobby

x x x x x x x x x x x x x x x x x x x x x x x x o o o o x x x x x x x x x x x x x x x x x x x x x x x x This is just a sample, baby!!!

November 3, 1945

Dearest Family,

I am getting mail quite regularly now. I sure am happy to hear from all of you, only I wish you wouldn't feel so bad about me being sent over here

to the O.A.F. I know when I first found out about it I
was pretty bitter, but now I'm reconciled to the fact
the Army cannot dispense with my services. Time is
passing fairly fast over here. Of course nothing like
it did when we were flying combat. This base was a
former Luftwaffe reconnaissance outfit. There are
burned jerry ships all around the field that testify to
the marksmanship of the American fighter pilots, to
whose ranks I must say I'm proud to belong.

You know that boy Mitchell I was telling you about
from St. Albans? (He's from up at two-mile and a
good friend of the Sidebottoms). Well, he got drunk
Sat. nite and threatened to kill another boy (who was
also looped) with a drawn pistol, over some kraut
slut. Well, I have both of them in the clunk awaiting
a court-martial. I hate to do it, because both of them
are psycho-neurotic and should be under medical
surveillance. I hate to throw the book at them, but
what can I do? Besides, the C.O. is pressing me to give
it to 'em. The C.O.'s a captain who volunteered for
regular Army and he's bucking for a major.

Mom, I gotta hand it to you for hornswaggling Pop
into getting breakfast. I only hope that you don't give
Evelyn too many pointers on how to handle us men.
Here we think that we're wearing the pants, and all the
time you gals are leading us around by the nose—and
how we love it.

About those trials of war criminals at Nuremberg,
I wouldn't stand a chance of getting in to hear them.
They're awfully strict about who gets in there, nobody
but the legal officers, workers and newspaper people.
Everyday they have the building guarded by tanks and
tommy-gun-armed guards, and the road is roped off
for blocks around. They aren't taking any chances on
anybody giving them any trouble.

Glad to hear that St. Albans beat Madison, and
I know Clate did a good job. I wouldn't worry about
his knees if nothing is wrong with the joints. As long
as the joints aren't chipped or any cartilage floating
around, there's nothing to worry about. Heck, a boy is
bound to get banged up a little playing football. But

Clayton, you remember this: the guys who get hurt
seriously, broken legs, twisted knees, etc. are the guys
who loaf and are not in good physical condition. As
long as you "put out," you'll be OK.

Hope to see you all soon. You just don't know how
homesick I am for Evelyn and all you folks. All my
love, Cobby

The Nuremberg War Trials of Nazi Leaders 1945-1949

Following the war, the Allies agreed that leaders responsible for the
horrendous atrocities against humanity, the Holocaust, should be brought
to justice through a judicial process. The city of Nuremberg, Germany, was
selected for the trials of major Nazi war criminals for practical and symbolic
reasons. The Palace of Justice, a place known for its infamous propaganda
Nazi rallies, was chosen for several reasons: there was sufficient office and
trial space available, an adjacent prison simplified custody of the accused,
and this complex had emerged intact following Allied bombing of the city.
The International Military Tribunal was made up of jurists from the Allied
countries of power, including the United States, Great Britain, France, and
the Soviet Union. The most famous trials of major war criminals took place
in 1945-46, although trials against Nazi leaders for war crimes, medical
experiments, and other atrocities against humanity continued until 1949.
According to information provided by the Museen der stadt Nurnberg, 24
of the 177 defendants were sentenced to death, 20 to life imprisonment and
98 to long-term prison sentences. There were several others who escaped
trial and punishment by taking their own lives.

Although Cobby flew over Nuremberg, he did not have an aerial
view of the Palace of Justice where the Nuremberg trials took place.
However, he made several good aerial photographs of Soldiers Field and
Soldiers Stadium, located on the other side of the city where annual Nazi
propaganda rallies were held. These huge choreographed events were
attended by thousands of soldiers filling the field to capacity and were used
to show the world the strength and might of Germany's military. Hitler's
speeches were broadcast around the world with films of this propaganda
event shown in newsreels that preceded movies in theatres.

"Soldiers Stadium and Soldiers Field" [Cobby Webb]

November 6, 1945

My Darling Evelyn,
    *What a beautiful day it is here in Germany. The sun
is shining brightly without a cloud in the sky. The only
thing that mars its perfect beauty is a slight haze, but
even that lends charm to the countryside.*
    *I've returned from a little scrounging expedition.
One of the outfits moved out and left a lot of kraut
furniture. So I got a couch and a few knick knacks
yesterday and today my M.P.'s got three more
davenports, a half dozen easy chairs and some tables
and drapes. We're furnishing one of the rooms here in
the guard house (not a cell) and we're going to make a
day room out of it and it should be pretty snazzy when
we finish. We bought a German radio that is really a lu
lu, and I'm sure we'll spend most of our time in there
reading and listening to programs from the states.*
    *We had a little excitement around here yesterday
afternoon. Two German girls were cleaning some clothes
with gasoline, 100 octane, which is like dynamite, in*

the boiler room. They had 10 gallons in two five gallon jerri cans. Well, the fumes got a little heavy and one of the cans exploded. And the two girls were burned pretty bad around the face, hands and legs. They ran out of the building and a polish D.P., a boy about 18, got a pail of water and threw it on the fire. Well, as you know, water is the worst thing that you can put on a gasoline fire because it just speeds the fire. When he threw the water on the fire the other can of gas exploded, and it was a dilly. I was in my room, just around the corner from where all this was taking place. And at the second explosion, fire came shooting under my door and scared about ten years outa me. Well I ran out in the hall where the flames and smoke were shooting out of the wash rooms like mad, and I heard this Polish boy yelling and pounding on the door trying to get outside. I called him and got him in my room. God what a sight, all the skin on his hands and face burned away and most of his hair. I threw a blanket around him (his clothes were smoldering) and took him over to the dispensary. There they bandaged him up and took him to the hospital. The fire fighters put the fire out with only a little damage. I guess I was the most excited guy on the field until I got hold of a bottle of cognac. Then, of course, I calmed right down. Everybody is going to be OK, but boy, was I scared at the time!

Well, Sweetheart, I guess I'd better close now. I can hardly wait until I get home. I keep thinking of what I'll do when I see you again for the first time in over a year. I hope that I'll be rational. Remember love o' my life—I'll love you forever, Cobby

November 10, 1945

Dearest Family,
This sure has been a dreary week in ole Bavaria. It's been rainy and steadily turning colder since

Monday. I wouldn't be at all surprised if it snowed this week-end. I'm sure glad that we have nice snug barracks. It sure would be terrible if we had to spend another winter in Nissen huts (prefabricated building of corrugated steel in the shape of a half cylinder). That's one good thing about the O.A.F. We have the best quarters, and the food can't be beat.

I had a little trouble this morning with some kraut. He came up here after some furniture that we had taken when one of the other outfits moved out. He had a letter from the Burgomeister (city Mayor) who said we had no right to the furniture. I asked who he thought won the war and threw him out. Boy, that burns me up. These damn Germans seem to think we owe them something. Then we caught a couple of Krauts stealing gasoline last Saturday night and we kept them over the week-end in our jail and turned them over on Monday to the Military Government. Both of them will probably get a year or two a piece. By golly, if I start having trouble this winter I'm going to shoot a few. I have quite an arsenal here at the Guardhouse anticipating such a day. I have about twelve .45's and four or five rifles and Carbines. But the best persuaders I have are a sawed off shotgun and a Thompson submachine gun. I was down at the range today shooting the Thompson sub machine gun. Frankly, I couldn't hit a bull in the rear with a handful of rice. But that thing sure kicks out enough lead to scare the hell out of anyone within a mile of it. In fact it would cut a man in two pieces if it ever hit him.

By dern, I wanta see ol' Clate play ball so bad I can taste it. Those accounts of his prowess on the gridiron sure do sound good. If he doesn't make all state I am personally going to clean up on a few sports writers. What do people around town think of him? I hope Clate's knees aren't serious. Gosh, take good care of those knees, Clate. They're your biggest worry playing football and college coaches hate to take ball players who have trick knees, especially backs. Well, I guess I'll stop now. All my love, Cobby

November 13, 1945

Hello Darling,

I've just come from the bar where I indulged in exactly two bourbons & cokes. Pretty good stuff. American you know. Reminds me of the good ol' days back in the states. Remember how Ernie Perry used to carry around a case of Tennessee mash bourbon in the back of his car?

I flew the cub for a couple of hours today, but the weather is getting so bad it is doubtful that I will fly much at all this month. I've made up my mind that I'm not going to fly any fighters 'cause the maintenance is so poor nowadays. Almost all of the crew chiefs have gone home and the fellows who are crewing the ships now are very inexperienced. Why, in the fighter group the pilots are taking care of the airplanes, pre-flighting them and warming them up etc., but not doing any technical work on them.

The Americans are beginning to have a little trouble with the krauts over here. Thursday night seven G.I.'s were killed in Frankfurt. The same night three had their throats slit in Ansbach. I've already told my M.P.'s to be more alert and to shoot first and ask questions later when they see a German lurking around the base at night. I'm going to requisition another submachine gun and more pistols, just in case there should be some real organized resistance on the part of the krauts. We have already started firing some of the Germans we have employed on the base. Right now the Germans out number the Americans about two to one, and if they ever organized, it would be pretty simple for them to seize the arms in the guys' rooms and take over the base. I kinda wish they would start something. There weren't enough of those blankety-blank krauts killed during the war. By golly, if I start having trouble this winter, I'm going to shoot a few. I'd feel more at ease.

I hope everything is OK with you, darling. I'm fine, only lonesome as the very devil. Sometimes I can hardly convince myself that you are my wife. That we will belong to each other as long as we live seems like a dream. I'm gonna have to get another heart to hold all the love I have for you. I'll try my best to make you the happiest girl in the world. Thru thick and thin, as long as I have you, I can never go wrong. I guess I kinda love you, Evelyn, and know I could never live without you.

Maybe if I'm lucky I can start school the second semester, sometime in February. But that means I'll have to get home the first of January, cause I wanta take a month long vacation to get used to being married again. I don't think I'll be away from you much longer. Well, sweetness, I guess I'd better sign off for now. I'll Love You Forever, Cobby

November 20, 1945

My Darling Evelyn,
I guess you're wondering why I haven't written you for the past few days. Well, baby, it's like this. Last Wednesday three of us got a wild hair up—and decided to go to Brussels for a few days, so right away we got orders cut for five days Temporary Duty in Belgium. So we took off Thursday morning in one of the German cars we have. Our first stop was Frankfurt. In case you didn't know, Frankfurt is where the Supreme Headquarters of the U.S. occupation forces is. I guess there are over a hundred generals in there, and the chicken is really terrific. One day I flew up there and they wouldn't let me in the mess hall because I didn't have a tie on. That's just an idea of the way they operate up there. Then we drove to Mainz and up the Rhine Valley to Cologne. It's really beautiful thru there. The road is right on the river and the hills tower on either side with castles on the peaks. Of course everything is all

beaten up with torn up roads and shelled and bombed buildings. The ride across the Cologne Plain was strewn with German and American tanks, American about 3 to 1. A lot of American boys lost their lives there. But speaking of war casualties, you should have seen Aachen and Duren. Duren especially. It was flattened to the ground and Aachen was almost as bad. Those krauts sure gave us some hard looks. We spent the night in Liege Belgium and shoved off the next day, going through Mons to see how our old field at Chievres Base was. Boy you could never recognize it. They've built buildings all over with heavy equipment parked there. Boy, was I surprised, it doesn't even look like an air field anymore.

We finally hit Brussels Friday afternoon. After we got our Belgium billets we were on our way to our hotel, when we got caught in a parade for Churchill. People were everywhere waiting to see him and it delayed us getting to our room by almost three hours. Boy, were we P. O. 'd!

Friday night we went to the U.S. Officers Leave Center. There we met a bunch of guys we knew, so the next three days were spent partying and talking over the good old days, when we flew missions almost every day, and had plenty of excitement to keep us on our toes. Well, we left early Monday morning and got as far as Frankfurt. At Frankfurt we stopped to have supper and when we got back in the car, the damned thing wouldn't start. (Oh, I forgot to tell you, the roads were so bad and we were in such a hurry that we had strewn parts all along the way.) So we got a push to the car park where we could leave the car all night under Army surveillance. If you don't keep an armed guard on the car at night, the damned krauts are liable to walk off with everything detachable. This morning we finally got the thing fixed. We needed a bunch of fuses and all the ignition wiring reconnected and got here around 1530 this afternoon. But all in all it was a swell trip and a good time was had by all.

I have a chance to play football with the 64th Fighter Wing All Stars, but I think I'm gonna turn it *down, 'cause I'm in such poor shape. If I play I'll have to have a couple of weeks to get back on the ball—that means I gotta quit smokin' and drinkin'. Too much trouble, besides it's not worth it.*

Well, dearest I'd better close now—I've rambled long enough. Remember my dearest, I'll love you forever,
Cobby

November 24, 1945

Dearest Family,

I'm sitting in my office this morning and I'm nearly frozen. It sure is cold over here. I'm surprised we haven't had half a dozen blizzards this week. We're having a pretty hard time with our coal and water. The heat is turned off at 1100 in the morning and turned off again at 1730 in the afternoon, goes off again at 2330 and doesn't come on until 0700. And we only have hot water four days a week. Starting Monday, the electricity is going to be shut off four hours each day. That's because we can't get enough diesel oil to run the generator. Things sure are getting rough in Germany. I'll sure be glad when I'm on that ol' boat sailing for the good old U.S.A.

I guess I may as well tell you about my accident. I turned over a jeep the other night. It wasn't wholly my fault because a big army truck ran me off the road into a ditch causing me to lose control of the jeep and turn over. That's another thing about a jeep—the wheel base is so short that they turn over easy. We had a wooden top on it, and that's what kept us from getting hurt. What gets me, is that's the first accident I've ever had, on the ground or in the air (pardon me while I knock on wood) and it spoils my good record.

Don't you all ever think that I'll get a promotion, because to get one you have to sign up for the regular army. And the three years I've been a guest of Uncle

Sam is enough for me. I'm sure looking forward to the day when I'll be able to step out in slacks and a sport coat, when I'll feel like an individual again, and won't have to say yessir to some crack trained officer who doesn't know sh__ from apple butter. The only thing I'll miss is the thrill of flying a "hot" ship.

We have a new C.O. for the field who's only been overseas a short time. Boy, is he eager! He's really been laying the law down and giving me a lot of regulations and new rules that he wants my military police to enforce. But I guess everything he is doing is for the best. The only thing that we fellows in the Service Group violently protest is the consolidation of the two mess halls and officers clubs. To date we have a very nice set up. There are only about twenty-five officers in the Service Group, and our food is terrific because the cooks can take pains with their cooking. That's all going to change now.

I sure like the idea of Clate and I playing ball for the same school, but I'm afraid that it's kinda impossible. When he gets out of high school, he'll have the chance to be a big shot at a big school because he's good enough. I want to go to a small school where I'll have a chance to play a little football. I'm not kidding myself. I know I'm not good enough for the big time, but he definitely is.

Well, I gotta go now. Hope to see you soon. All my love, Cobby

November 25, 1945

My Darling,

I'm sitting in my office, right smack dab on the radiator. I'm freezing. By dern, it's cold over here. I'll sure be glad when I have you to snuggle up to again. This sleeping alone is for the birds. Besides I get cold and my blankets aren't sufficient. Please Ma'am, do you think you could write to the President and ask him to send me you, or send you me. I'd sure appreciate it, and tell him if he will, we both will vote for him in the next election. OK, Sweet.

Boy! Am I P.O.'d—I've been giving these krauts hell all day, especially the women. They seem to think that just because they're shacking up with the G.I.'s, they can have any and everything they want. I've been kicking them off the field all day. There's nothing that makes me as mad as a woman who thinks she can get anything she wants with a flip of her butt. Thank God, they're firing most of the Germans who work here on the base.

Now that I've got that out of my system, I will turn to a more pleasant subject. I got the best ol' letter from you today written ten short days ago. I can just close my eyes and see you writing it all propped up in bed, with your hair all rolled up and lotion all over your face. Baby, you know all that doesn't make any difference to me. Why, I'd love you if you were bald (heaven forbid) and didn't have any teeth. You know, I like to watch you when you're asleep. You look so peaceful and calm, just like a baby. It does something to me. Makes my heart feel like it's going to burst. I don't know how to explain it, but it's a wonderful feeling. Yes darling, I've thought about what would have happened if I hadn't gone to that U.S.O. dance and met you. And I shudder to think that maybe I'd gone all through life not knowing or loving you. I'm sure glad I like to dance!

I got a letter from one of my buddies who was in my old outfit back in England, name's Jim Hurly. He's in a convalescent hospital in San Antonio, getting some plastic surgery done on his lip. He got shot up one day and had to make a crash landing, and it banged him up a little. But to get on with what he had to say. He's sorta disgusted with things back in the states, and he is going to try and stay in the Army and come back over here. He said he missed the old gang something fierce. But he is single, and didn't have you to come back to like I do. I can't get over it, he's the second guy (buddy) I've heard from who's gone home, and wished he was back with the fellows. We sure did have a terrific outfit back there in

England. And I have every intention of introducing you to them in the future.

Oh, Pop wrote and told me how he had gotten a ration slip for three new tires back in December and how he neglected getting them in hopes he could buy them wholesale. Well, now that tire rationing is all finished he can't buy any tires anywhere. That's what he gets for trying to swing a "deal."

Well, sweetheart, I guess I'd better close now. Remember, Evelyn dearest, my heart is at your feet.
Cobby

December 2, 1945

Dearest Family,

Just got back from taking a nice shower. It's shower day today, you know. Every other day the water is hot and you gotta jump in the shower room before it gets cold. Another week has gone by and that means one less week that I have to stay in this place. I have been getting quite a few boxes lately. I got one this week from you all with the shaving cream in it. Thanks a lot. I've been getting cigs like mad, and I have about six or seven cartons now. Don't send any more cigarettes or candy.

We are still having trouble with these dern krauts. Lately we've had a lot of drugged-up women with syphilis and clap, sometimes with both. We have to lock up a couple of women every night for slipping through the fence and staying all night. We turn'em all over to the Military Government, and they send them to hospitals (civilian) and cure'em, then lock'em up for a while. The VD rate is increasing everyday and since the medics started using penicillin, they have more cases. I guess the guys aren't careful when it can be cured so easily.

Then I had some trouble with a kraut in Erlangen yesterday. We took over one of our jeeps to get winterized. When we got back, our jeep was shy a tire, a five gallon can full of gas, and the lousy bastards drained about 8 gallons out of the tank. Besides that, they stole some plywood we gave them to cover our jeep with. We took the head man to Military Government, and I don't know what they will do with him.

Otherwise, I don't do a thing anymore but dream of Evelyn and home. I'm trying to figure out what I'm going to say when I first see all of you again. I don't doubt a bit that all I'll be able to do is stand and grin at you all. I know I won't be able to say anything, but I'm hoping to be seeing you soon. All my love, Cobby

December 24, 1945

Dearest Family,

Before I start this I want to wish you all a very
Merry Christmas and a Happy New Year. Well, at last I
have something definite about going home. The point
score for officers drops to 70 points as of the 31st of
December, at which time yours truly becomes eligible
for the ol' boat trip. I doubt very seriously whether I
leave here before the 10th or 15th of January. In either
case don't expect me in the states until the middle of
February. I'll wire you or call you as soon as I hit the
U.S.A.

I've been thinking of you all and Evelyn. How
lucky I am to get a wife like Evy. I'm still amazed at my
good fortune. But as you say, Pop, good judgment for
picking gals comes natural, look what you got! Yep.
Sure glad that I have a wife and won't have to carry a
club to beat off the gals anymore.

I'm getting pretty excited about the prospects of
leaving here for the U.S.A. I want to spend the first
few days at home with Evelyn, so I can get used to
being married again. I know if I don't, neither one of
us will be very good company to you all, because we
will be too interested in each other. I know you all will
understand how I feel. Evelyn wrote and told me she
had saved about $2500 since I have been over here, and
by the time I get home with the money I've saved over
here, I figure we will have $3500 to start our married
life with. When I go to school, I'll get $90 a month
under the G.I. Bill of Rights. The only thing about
going to school which is worrying me, is I don't have
the slightest idea what I want to take.

Dad, I haven't lost my football confidence, I've just
lost interest in football. It doesn't seem as important
as it did before I came over here. Of course, when I get
back to school, things might change. I'm planning on
having a talk with Sid Aidman when I get back and see
what he thinks about a busted down ex pilot playing
a little ball on scholarship. Clate, congratulations

on being the leading scorer in the Kanawha Valley
Conference. How's your chances at All State, do you
know? I'm pulling for you, boy.

I didn't tell you about not being the Provost
Marshall any more, did I? Well, last Friday a joker
came into the group who has been an M.P. officer for
two years. And being as he's regular Army, he took
over. I'm Communication officer, which is just a title.
I don't have much to do anymore. So I'm spending
most of my time getting all my stuff together for going
home. 'Course I get quite a bit of sleeping, too.

I took off yesterday in a fifty-one to fly down and
have a look at the Alps. Well, when I started back,
my compass went out, and I got lost, and ended up
landing over near Wurzburg. It was too late to come
on home, and besides I couldn't get any gas right
away. So I stayed there all night. What a deal, I've
never spent a more miserable night since I've been in
Germany. I slept on a pile of logs. At least that's what it
felt like, and it was cold. Here I am shivering like a dog
sitting on a corn cob, with only two blankets. As you
can readily understand, I didn't sleep too well. Besides
that, I couldn't find the mess, so I went without
breakfast, and then I had to wait two hours on some
gas. God, what an experience, but that is my last ride
in a P-51, so I don't mind.

I guess St. Albans lost quite a few boys in this
war. I just thank God that I was spared. But I don't
guess my number was up. Sure was too bad about
Patton kicking off, wasn't it? The army sure lost one
of its greatest Generals. I think he would have pulled
through OK if age hadn't been against him.

Well, I'll close now, got to do a little work around
here. Remember folks, don't worry about me, I'll be
home before you know it. All my love, Cobby

December 24, 1945

My Darling Evelyn,

Here it is Christmas Eve, and I'm afraid I'm just a little blue today. Dammit, the next war I'm in, I sure am going to take you along! I have some news for you today—we got in the new officers yesterday, and that means we're going home pretty soon. All of the boys, with sixty-five or more points got an assistant. I have a deputy sheriff now. I brought him over to the guard house this morning and right now he's looking through files. The latest rumor is that all officers with over 65 points will be on their way home by the 1st of January. Keep your fingers crossed, my darling.

Baby, I think you've done a wonderful job with our savings. After all, I've only been over here a year and you've saved $2500 of the allotments alone. We should get about $725 in war bonds that will be worth $1000 in ten years, and I'll bring a little money home with me. You know we're worth quite a bit of money. By golly, Evelyn, I sure am proud of you. I sure am lucky to have a gal who is as beautiful as you and with brains, too!

Say, did you get that gown and slip I sent to you? I have an American parachute over here, and I'm trying to get up enough nerve to include it when I send your boots. Parachute silk is better for nightgowns than chiffon. 'Course you can almost see everything thru this silk. It's really almost as sheer as hose. I'll bet you'd like some undies and stuff made out of it. I'll try to get my nerve up.

All this talk about diaphragms, inserters, etc. sorta embarrasses me. I don't know anything about them, or how they're used. I guess you'll have to explain the details when I get home. So you think Jackie's marriage is just a sex affair. Well, you gotta admit baby, sex is a very interesting sideline of marriage. And I don't believe that either you or I are lacking when it comes to sex. But as far as I'm concerned, I'd just as soon not call our lovemaking sex, because "sex" to me is a word which denotes a very squalid and illicit relationship, whereas our sexual relationship is something beautiful and to be cherished forever.

Well, I guess I better close now. Give my love to Mama and Pappy and to you my sweet. All my love forever, Cobby

P.S. I'm enclosing another picture of me. Don't worry. I'm only sitting and not riding. Don't know how to ride a motorcycle and don't care to learn.

January 1, 1946

Dearest Family,

Happy New Year! Not much doing around here last night—no party, no celebration, no nothing, except that some of the guys shot off their forty-fives at midnight.

I haven't been doing much today. Didn't get up until about 10:30, moped around until lunch, ate, took a shower, shaved and dressed up and now I'm writing you. Oh yes, I went over to the library and found a couple of books to read and am planning to have a rip-roaring time. Well, the books are western stories!

I hope you had a nice Christmas. As you probably know, mine wasn't so hot. It didn't even seem like Christmas, and I was very thankful because I would have been even more homesick.

Our date of departure has been set back until around January 20th or maybe a few days before. This setback is due to the bad weather on the Atlantic, so I guess all there is to do but wait.

Well, I'll close now. Remember folks, don't worry about me, I'll be home before you know it. All my love, Cobby

January 7, 1946

Hello Darling,

Another day and no mail, no mail from you or anyone, but all of us are in the same boat. There just hasn't been any coming through. I saw in the "Stars and Stripes" where a C-54 crashed and 4,000 pounds of incoming mail was burned. That happened about four or five days ago.

Well, I got some hot poop tonight. You probably know about the "Point System" being abolished. Today over the radio they claimed that the "Point System" and length of service will still determine who goes home under this new deal. A teletype came through today, and men with 71 points are leaving here the end of January and will be on the boat by the first of February! I have 70. God, what I would give for one measly little point. I guess that I'll make it sometime in February, but doubt I get home before March.

Today up at Wing Headquarters in Frankfurt, our immediate command, there was a big demonstration by 3500 GI's marching to protest the new re-deployment plan. Windows were broken in the General's office and everything! Boy! All the boys over here are P.O.'d and bitter. Everyone is dissatisfied about the way things are being run over here. Honest to God, you never saw such inefficiency in all your life. The Germans are getting away with everything and all the Army does is shrug its shoulders. And it's all because these pompous asses up in higher headquarters are so scared if they don't keep everyone, or at least enough to have normal strength in their outfits, they will be demoted to their permanent rank. That means Generals could be reduced two grades and the same applies to majors and colonels. They claim there is a shortage of officers over here, but there are so many on this field they are stumbling over each other. When I get home, I'll explain to you what was driving your ol' man nuts in Germany.

Well, Baby, I'd better close before I get all lit up and blow my stack. One thing for sure, I'll never enlist in another Army. They will have to scour the hills of West Virginia to find me in the draft! I'll love you always, Evelyn. Cobby

It had been a long year for Cobby, and his frustration and disappointment are understandable as he keeps missing the boat for home by a point or two. It is also understandable that evacuating over one million military personnel following a war of this magnitude and maintaining a permanent occupation force in Europe is a very complicated process. Prior to January the rate in which soldiers were sent home was based on an individual "Points System." However, in January 1946, the need for a permanent occupation force of 300,000 soldiers became the controlling factor, and the rate of sending veterans home slowed down. Interestingly, a monthly demobilization "slow down" meant that beginning in January until July, 50,000 soldiers from the European Theatre would be shipped home each month with a total of 300,000 soldiers deployed in a six-month period.

January 31, 1946

Dearest Family,
I believe that within the next two weeks I'll have my orders to leave or be on my way. If that's the case, you can expect to see me before the 15th of March. I'll cable you when I leave this station.
By the way, before I forget it, thank you all for the lovely birthday card you sent. I find it pretty hard to realize that I'm now 22 years old. I feel the same as I did when I was 20.
In this letter I'm enclosing $400 worth of money orders. I'd like for you to cash them and put them in the bank in my name, please. I'll probably send you

some more in a few days. This dough is going to be my honeymoon fund, and I'm going to have quite a time!

Hey Pop, you remember when I asked you to keep an eye out for a good bargain on a used car? I'm determined that I'm going to get a car of my own. I think I'll either get a Chevy or a Ford, a club coupe with a steel top. No convertibles for this kid! I had to laugh, Pop, when you said you hadn't the nerve to do 30 in our car anymore. I agree with you. I feel much safer in the air doing 500 mph than I do on the ground doing 30. I guess it's because I have more room upstairs.

I think I'll sign off now. I'm gonna take a shower and clean up for dinner. Be back as soon as I finish—

Well, here I am back again. Just shaved, showered and shampooed. Feel like a million bucks. Now if there was only someplace to go and something to do. Hope to be seeing you all soon, in about a month. All my love, Cobby

P.S. Don't forget to deposit the money for me. I'm going to need it.

February 5, 1946

Dearest Darling,

By the time you get this letter, I should be on my way home. The long awaited day has finally arrived. A teletype came in tonight saying all the 71 pointers will be leaving this field on the 7th of February. That's day after tomorrow. I have a busy day ahead of me as I've gotta get my 4 hours flying time and clear the field, besides turning in my flying equipment and packing. Our group will go by truck to the coast to get on a boat for home. I don't care if I get seasick, I've been homesick for so long. Oh yes, Evy, I'll cable you when I leave to tell you I'm on my way, and I'll call you as soon as I get to the states. As soon as you get my cable, quit your job,

248

pack up and take off for West Virginia! I should be home sometime the first week of March.

I've been thinking about how I'm going to act when I first see you, and I get a weak and fluttery feeling down deep inside. It's the most wonderful feeling.

We'll meet in Charleston, baby, and I'll tell you what I thought we'd do. If in the daytime, we'll go home with the folks and then to the Bridal Suite at the Daniel Boone. If at night, we'll go straight to the Daniel Boone and spend about three or four days alone, just the two of us! Gol dernit, I wish I was stepping off that train right this minute.

Don't worry about not being able to say anything when we first see each other. Just be there in my arms, and we'll think of something to say in a couple of days. You know, I think you're about the smartest gal alive, besides being the most beautiful.

Looking back over the past fourteen months, I don't see how I've been able to stand being away from you so long. You can bet your boots that you won't be outa my sight a minute when I get back. There are so many things I want to say to you, Evelyn, and 99 out of 100 are I love you. I'll see you soon and I'll love you forever. Cobby

February 14, 1946

Dearest Pop & Fritzi,

I'm a mighty excited girl tonight! I had a telegram from Cobby & he said their movement orders had come in & that'll put him in the states the first week of March! Isn't it wonderful? Golly — I just can't believe it. He wants me to meet him in St. Albans. I think he said he'd probably be sent to a camp in Pennsylvania after the ship gets to New York & then he'd get a train right through Washington & on to West Virginia! Goodness — I'm so excited I can barely write. Won't it just be grand? I just can hardly wait to see that boy!

I sure am hoping Cobby will be able to get the gas, so we Webbs can invade Nashville. Goodness—we're gonna have so much fun! Love, Evey

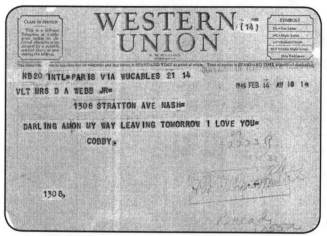

DARLING AM ON MY WAY LEAVING TOMORROW I LOVE YOU = COBBY

It would take two weeks to cross the ocean by ship and another week to process out of the Army. Cobby would arrive by train in Charleston, West Virginia.

REFERENCES

[1] "Point System." The Strictly G.I. Website. Accessed September 2, 2012. http://users.skynet.be/jeeper/point.html

[2] "Potsdam Conference." The Encyclopædia Britannica Online Website. Accessed September 25, 2012 from http://www.britannica.com/EBchecked/topic/472799/Potsdam-Conference

3   "MILESTONES: 1937-1945: The Potsdam Conference." The Official Website of the U.S. Department of State Office of the Historian Website. Accessed December 12, 2012. http://history.state.gov/milestones/1937-1945/PotsdamConf

4   "Nuremberg Trials." The United States History Website. Accessed September 11, 2012. http:/ /www.u-s-history.com/pages/h1685.html

5   "The Historical Venue: Memorium Nuremberg Trials." The Official website of museen der stadt Nurnberg. Accessed October 12, 2012. http://www.memorium-nuremberg.de/history/historical-venue.html

6   "The Historical Venue: Memorium Nuremberg Trials." The Official website of museen der stadt Nurnberg. Accessed October 12, 2012. http://www.memorium-nuremberg.de/history/historical-venue.html

CHAPTER THIRTEEN

Homecoming, March 7, 1946

St. Albans, West Virginia. Evelyn opened her eyes, blinked a couple of times to focus, and checked the clock again on the bedside table. It was three—too early to get out of bed. She couldn't sleep. Cobby was coming home today.

Evelyn had waited a long time for this moment, and the six months following the war's official end had been, in many ways, the hardest. She had first hoped and expected that Cobby would be home in early fall, after the war ended, and then no later than Thanksgiving, but the holidays passed, and orders kept changing. So when Evelyn received that long-awaited cable three weeks ago, it seemed unreal. She had gone through some big changes in the last three weeks—quitting her job, saying goodbye to friends and family, and preparing to leave her mother. This morning Evelyn felt a range of emotions from joy and excitement to nervousness and fear, as she thought about her three-year-long relationship with Cobby. In three years, they had been together in the same town less than five months, but had shared their lives and feelings on paper, writing to each other. The letters they exchanged connected them across the miles and through time.

Evelyn wondered if Cobby would be the same person she fell in love with or if he'd been hardened and changed by the experiences of war. It was another risk, just like the night on the train platform as she was leaving for Nashville and Cobby convinced her to stay and marry him that night. She recalled that those first three months they were able to spend together were the happiest days of her life. Evelyn smiled to herself. Her heart was so full of love it might just jump out of her chest. With that, she calmed her inner fears and drifted back to sleep.

A little while later, Fritzi made her way to the kitchen to put on a pot of coffee. She stood at the sink peering out the window into the darkness of this pre-dawn morning. The house was still and quiet. Fritzi didn't care about sleeping. She preferred to spend some time alone to think about her first-born son and the blessing of his homecoming. Although the last year had been fraught with worry, Fritzi had always believed in her heart that Cobby would return, despite the fact that other friends and families in St. Albans had faced the deaths of their beloved sons, fathers, and brothers. Fritzi had refused to live in fear, and her headstrong personality and determination combined with an inner strength and faith had always guided her life. Cobby possessed similar personality qualities, combined with a joy of living and optimism that had always made his daily life an adventure. Fritzi beamed in the moonlight and was grateful that this day had finally arrived.

Evelyn, wrapped in a robe, joined Fritzi in the kitchen. They took their cups of hot coffee and Lucky Strike cigarettes and moved to the screened-in front porch and the comfortable rocking chairs, where they watched the night turn into day. Mother and daughter-in-law could barely contain their excitement. Both talkers, they began chatting as they sipped their coffee, although it is doubtful either one actually heard what the other one said. It was a monumental day, and the nights of wonder and worry were over!

Within an hour, Pop, a stoic, rather serious man had a bounce in his step as he wandered around the house with an energy that kept him moving room to room.

Clayton was only fourteen when Cobby left home for the Army, and now he was no longer the "little" brother, but a tall, well-developed high school football star with dreams and aspirations to be an All American football player in college. Clayton wondered if he was "old enough" to be Cobby's "friend" and not just his little brother, especially since they both loved football. Clayton would be leaving in the summer to play football at the University of Kentucky under the direction of Coach Paul "Bear Bryant", and he hoped Cobby might even consider going to school with him at UK. He couldn't wait to see Cobby—there was so much to talk about.

Although Charleston, West Virginia, was only fifteen miles from St. Albans, the Webb family left for the Charleston Railroad Station several hours ahead of time. It was not a large terminal, but it was an extremely busy place with soldiers returning home.

The Webb family navigated through a sea of men in military uniforms, all looking alike, as families scrambled to find their loved one. Evelyn's heart was in her throat as she scanned the train looking for a tall handsome man—the love of her life. Fritzi and Pop were anxiously searching the crowd for their son. All the worries of the last few years had been washed away by joy, now shining on the faces of the Webb family as they paraded single file through the crowds.

Evelyn saw him first. She captured a glimpse of Cobby as he stood in the doorway of the train looking over the crowd before stepping down on the platform. He was wearing his Army uniform and carrying a large duffle bag.

Cobby's face broke into a broad grin when he saw a petite woman with long chestnut brown hair darting around people and running in his direction. He stepped off the platform and in one sweeping motion dropped his bag and picked up Evelyn off the ground and kissed her long and hard. Then with one arm still around Evelyn, he reached for his mother, his family, and held them close. There was laughter, there were tears of joy and relief as this family huddled together with their arms wrapped around one another in a tight circle.

I don't know how long they hugged or how long they stood crying together that day, but for that moment, life was better than it had ever been before.

The war was over. Cobby was home at last.

The ending of one chapter in life was now the beginning of another. With the help of Coach Paul "Bear" Bryant, Cobby entered the University of Kentucky later that year, and he and Evelyn embarked on a marriage journey filled with love, laughter, and devotion. Their union was completed by a daughter in 1948, followed by twin sons in 1950. The war years had made them strong and able to endure and had taught them how beautiful it is to stay together, stay close, and hold each other up.

These two soul mates would share a deep love and eleven years of happiness before his untimely death in June, 1955. Cobby had told Evelyn in a letter dated July 15, 1944, "You're a part of me that will only die when I do." Yet I imagine Evelyn continued to feel his love through the veil between life and beyond. And she held tightly to her love for him and treasured the time they'd shared. She'd see their love forever in the faces of their children and grandchildren.

The flames of the undying love between Cobby and Evelyn will burn forever in the hearts of those left behind.

"Together at last"

High Flight

Oh! I have slipped the surly bonds of earth
And danced the skies on laughter-silvered wings;
Sunward I've climbed, and joined the tumbling mirth
Of sun-split clouds—and done a hundred things
You have not dreamed of—wheeled and soared and swung
High in the sunlit silence. Hov'ring there,
I've chased the shouting wind along, and flung

My eager craft through footless halls of air,
Up, up the long, delirious, burning blue
I've topped the wind-swept heights with easy grace
Where never lark, or even eagle flew—
And, while with silent lifting mind I've trod
The high untrespassed sanctity of space,
Put out my hand and touched the face of God.

John Gillespie Magee, Jr., 1941

Courtesy of National Museum of the U.S. Air Force

THE END